FOCUS
ON FACT

BY John F. MacArthur, Jr.

Keys to Spiritual Growth
Focus on Fact

FOCUS ON FACT

Why You Can Trust the Bible

John F. MacArthur, Jr.

Fleming H. Revell Company
Old Tappan, New Jersey

Scripture quotations not otherwise identified are from the King James Version of the Bible.

Scripture quotations identified NAS are from the New American Standard Bible, Copyright © THE LOCKMAN FOUNDATION 1960, 1962, 1963, 1968, 1971, 1972, 1973, and are used by permission.

Scripture quotations identified RSV are from the Revised Standard Version of the Bible, copyrighted 1946, 1952, © 1971 and 1973.

Library of Congress Cataloging in Publication Data

MacArthur, John, date
    Focus on fact.

    1. Bible—Evidences, authority, etc. 2. Bible—
Inspiration. I. Title.
BS480.M2   220.1   77-21755
ISBN 0-8007-0885-7

TO
Burton Michaelson, my friend,
who has given much of his life
to provide the place where
for nine years I have taught
the truths of the Holy Book

Contents

Preface

Is it easy to convince someone that the Bible is the Word of God on the basis of its unity, its scientific and historical accuracy, its miracles, and its archaeological evidence? I haven't found that to be the case. In a special series spread over a three-week period I presented such data at a private college in California. I thought the proof was overwhelming yet not one person became a believer. Why doesn't it convince all unbelievers when it is so convincing to us?

The reason unbelievers cannot accept legitimate and forceful proof is that they are blind to it. As the Apostle Paul wrote, "The natural man receiveth not the things of the Spirit of God: for they are foolishness unto him: neither can he know them, because they are spiritually discerned" (1 Corinthians 2:14). Only when the Holy Spirit does His regenerating work—only as He opens the mind, tears off the scales of blindness, gives life where there is death, and plants the marvelous understanding of the revelation of God—only then do people come to believe in and trust the Bible. The reason I know the Bible is true is that the Spirit of God has convinced me of it.

In light of this, I suggest a change in our approach. We have been saying, "Prophecy has been fulfilled. The Bible is scientifically accurate. Miracles occurred. The Bible produces radical and revolutionary changes in lives. Therefore, it is the Word of God." Instead, I propose that we declare, "The Bible *is* the Word of God. *Therefore,* prophecy has been fulfilled, miracles have taken place, scientific statements are correct, and lives have been transformed."

I am often asked what I believe about the Bible. Since I spend most of my life studying it, discussing it, teaching it, preaching it, writing about it, memorizing it, and endeavoring to live by it—that is a fair question. I should have some conviction about it and I do.

I believe the Bible is the only book ever written by the one God of the universe, who wrote it to reveal Himself to humanity. I believe the Bible is the only authoritative and absolutely reliable source of revelation from God with regard to the origin of man, his deliverance, his salvation, the moral and spiritual standards he is to live by, and his ultimate destiny. I also believe that the Bible is true in every detail, even to the very words in the original manuscripts. God wrote it—every word.

That is what I believe. This book is primarily for you who share that belief and who also love the Lord Jesus Christ. I write to strengthen your faith. I want you to see what a marvelous book the Bible is. I want you to get more confidence in it—to believe it with your whole heart. Then when someone says, "Why do you believe the Bible?" you will be able to give him your convincing reasons for the hope that is in you.

And in case there may be some of you who do not yet believe the Bible, I pray that you, too, will see what a marvelous book it is, and come to believe as you read this declaration of its incredible truthfulness.

FOCUS
ON FACT

1

The God Who Speaks

All mankind is trapped on planet earth, bounded by time and space and surrounded by an endless universe. And many sense in the deepest parts of their beings that somewhere out there is some kind of ultimate power or God. And so they try to discover how they can know this Supreme Being. The result is religion, the invention of man in his attempt to find God.

Christianity, however, teaches that we don't find God because God has already found us. He disclosed who He is. In the Old and New Testaments of Holy Scripture we have the total unveiling of God.

He Is There and He Is Not Silent. The Bible bridges a period of at least fifteen hundred years. During those long centuries God was always disclosing Himself because it is in His very nature to communicate. An artist paints and a singer sings because that is what is in them. God speaks because that is the natural thing for Him to do. He cannot remain undisclosed. Francis Schaeffer is right when he says of God, "He is there, and He is not silent." He cannot be silent.

In the beginning God spoke out of nothing and the universe was born. Through history He spoke to Abraham, to Moses, and to the prophets. For this reason, the Jews understood God as a speaking God, and through His messengers they often heard the expression "Thus saith the Lord." When Jesus came into the world, He was called the Word. It was the best title John could come up with for the revelation of God in the flesh—the living Word.

What God speaks *stays* spoken. "For ever, O Lord, thy word is settled in heaven" (Psalms 119:89). Jesus said, "Heaven and earth shall pass away, but my words shall not pass away" (Matthew 24:35). And Peter wrote, "The word of the Lord endureth for ever . . ." (1 Peter 1:25).

When God Is Silent, Watch Out.   The God who speaks, however, sometimes chooses to remain silent for a time. And when He does, it is always in judgment. For a long period, for example, God freely communicated with King Saul. But Saul's repeated rejection of the Lord and his frequent disobedience finally caught up with him. Then when Saul called upon the Lord, he received no answer (*see* 1 Samuel 28:6).

There came a time when God's patience with Israel was exhausted. He told His weeping prophet, Jeremiah, "Pray not for this people . . . . I will not hear their cry . . ." (Jeremiah 14:11, 12).

In the Book of Proverbs God promised to pour out His Spirit and to make known His words (*see* Proverbs 1:23). But what happens to those who refuse to listen? We are not left to guess.

> Because I called, and you refused; I stretched out my hand, and no one paid attention; And you neglected all my counsel, And did not want my reproof; I will even laugh at your calamity; I will mock when your dread comes, When your dread comes like a storm, And your calamity comes on like a whirlwind, When distress *and* anguish come on you. Then they will call on me, but I will not answer; They will seek me diligently, but they shall not find me.
>
> Proverbs 1:24–28 NAS

God freely shares Himself. But if we reject Him, that's it.

God Is Not a Floating Fog.   "What is He like—this Revealer who speaks?" you might wonder. Four things may be said. First, the God who speaks is personal. He calls Himself "I" and addresses us as "you." Moses inquired of God as to His name. "And God said unto Moses, I AM THAT I AM: and he said, Thus shalt thou say unto the children of Israel, I AM hath sent me unto you" (Exodus 3:14).

"I AM" indicates personality. God Himself had a name, even as He gave names to others—to Abraham, to Israel, and to the Jews. The name "I AM" stands for a free, purposeful, self-sufficient personality. God is what He wants to be, and He tells us that by His choice of a name.

God is not a floating fog. He is not an "it." He is not an aimless, blind force. He is not a cosmic energy. God is an almighty, self-existing, self-determining being with mind and will. He is a person!

If you read through the Bible long enough, you find out that God is not only personal but that He is also tripersonal. In the opening words of Genesis God said, "Let us make man in *our* image, after *our* likeness" (Genesis 1:26, author's italics). Then later, in the Psalms, we have a record of God speaking to God: "The *Lord* said unto my Lord . . ." (Psalms 110:1, author's italics). The New Testament name for God is "Father, Son, and Holy Spirit" (*see* Matthew 28:19). Mark it down: *God is personal.*

There Is a High Cost to Low Living.   There is a second thing about the Revealer God. He is moral. He reveals Himself as one supremely concerned about right and wrong. Morality is a high priority with God. That is wonderfully expressed in God's words to Moses: ". . . The Lord God, merciful and gracious, longsuffering, and abundant in goodness and truth, Keeping mercy for thousands, forgiving iniquity and transgression and sin, and that will by no means clear the guilty . . ." (Exodus 34:6, 7).

That may seem contradictory. After speaking of His grace, mercy, and forgiveness, God says that He won't let the guilty go. That means that God is a just God, and that He will not merely say to guilty people, "Well, it's all right. I'll let you off the hook." God does show mercy, but somebody has to pay the penalty for sin. The Gospels make it clear that the "someone" is Jesus Christ.

Getting to Know the Unknown God.   There is a third thing to be said about the personal nature of God. Not only is He personal and moral but He is also the source, the maintenance, and the end of all creation. In the words of Romans 11:36, "Of him, and through him, and to him are all things."

For an illustration, look and listen over the shoulder of Paul as he addresses the Athenians on Mars Hill. In Acts 17 Paul said, "Fellows, as I was coming into your city, I noted all the religious statues you have about. Obviously, you're a pretty religious bunch. I even found one statue dedicated to the 'Unknown God.' Well, I would like you to meet Him. I know Him very well" (*see* Acts 17:23).

Paul told them that God was the source of everything: "God that made the world and all things therein, seeing that he is Lord of heaven and earth . . ." (Acts 17:24). God also sustains everything, ". . . seeing he giveth to all life, and breath, and all things" (verse 25). God's sustaining power is expressed graphically in verse 28: "For in him we live, and move, and have our being . . . ." And God is the end, the goal, the purpose of all things: "That they should seek the Lord, if haply they might feel after him, and find him . . ." (verse 27).

Man's destiny is to seek and to know this God who gives life and who sustains life. The whole purpose of man's existence is fulfilled only when he knows God.

God Is Available to You.   All this is impressive, but it would not mean much unless one other thing were true: the God who speaks must be available to you. That is the whole purpose of His self-revelation. He wants you to know Him. Because God is a person He wants to have fellowship with you. The fact that He is moral indicates that He wants to deal with you righteously. The fact that He is the source, the sustainer, and the end of all creation means that your destiny is dependent upon your relationship to Him. And the fact that He is available to you is the concluding, exciting concept. You can come into a full relationship with the God who speaks—but the only place you can do that is in the pages of His revelation, the Bible.

2

God Has Spoken—
But How?

The God who speaks has done so in His revelation to us, the Bible. But how has God spoken? It is important that we know because much supposed revelation is being claimed today.

After I had spoken at a seminar, a young lady came up to me and asked, "You don't believe there is any more revelation being given today, do you?"

"No," I replied, "I believe the revelation of God has been completed. It is finished."

"Well, I happen to go to a church where we have an apostle," she insisted.

"That's very interesting. Who is he—Peter, James, John, or Paul?"

"Oh, he's not any of those, but he is an apostle."

"How do you know he is an apostle?"

"Because he speaks direct revelation from God."

I blinked. "You mean, when he gets up and talks, it isn't just a sermon, but it's God speaking through him?"

"That's right. He gives direct revelations every Sunday."

How can we evaluate a statement such as that? What shall we think when we go to a Christian bookstore and pick up a book that claims to be a revealed vision from God yet contradicts or adds to the Bible?

For the answer, we must look to the origin of the supposed message. Did it come from God's free, voluntary act of love in disclosing Himself to men, or did it come from the mind of a person who thought something ought to be said?

Did Moses one day, having nothing better to do, suddenly decide that he would record the creation of he world? "Now, let's see. I wonder how this whole thing came about. It seems to me that . . . ."

No! That's not how it happened. God told Moses what had occurred, and Moses in obedience sat down and recorded what had been divinely revealed to him: "In the beginning God created the heaven and the earth" (Genesis 1:1). This is revelation from God, not supposition from Moses.

Imagine Isaiah sitting down to write, "Therefore the Lord himself shall give you a sign; Behold, a virgin shall conceive, and bear a son, and shall call his name Immanuel" (Isaiah 7:14). I couldn't come up with that, but Isaiah did because it was revealed to him.

Imagine Micah saying, "Thou, Bethlehem, though thou be little among the sons of Judah, out of thee shall he come forth who is to be ruler over my people Israel" (*see* Micah 5:2). He couldn't have made any such valid prophecy unless it had been revealed to him.

Can you imagine David penning Psalm 22 and giving us an absolutely perfect description of the Crucifixion, even to the statement in verse 1, "My God, my God, why hast thou forsaken me?" and doing it hundreds of years before Jesus was born, and not having had it revealed to him by God?

The great prophecies written in the Bible came from God, not from men. They were God's thoughts, not the speculations of men.

The World of Nature.   God has revealed Himself to us in two broad categories. The first is through "natural" revelation. You can't look at the wonderful things you can see in the daytime, nor can you look at the stars of the nighttime without concluding that Somebody made it all—not and keep your mental sanity and balance. *Everything* cries out to the existence of God and His work.

A New Testament reference tells us what the revelation in creation communicates: "For the invisible things of him from the creation of the world are clearly seen, being understood by the things that are made, even his eternal power and

Godhead; so that they are without excuse" (Romans 1:20).

The world of nature reveals three things. The first is God's power. When we look at the created world, we can only stand in awe of the tremendous power that must have been exerted in its formation. Recently I read in two issues of the *National Geographic* articles about the sun and the movement of the stars and planets. Just one star, Betelgeuse, is twice the size of the earth's orbit around the sun and is 500 light-years away. At 186,000 miles per second, it takes 500 years for its light to reach the earth. It is just on the edge of the endless universe with billions of stars like it. And all were made by God!

The second thing nature tells us about is the Godhead. The Greek word has reference to His divine character. The God who created is the God in charge. He runs the show. He is in control of the universe.

Third, nature tells us of God's wrath. We infer that from the closing part of Romans 1:20, which says that the heathen are "without excuse." That is evident from the fact that everywhere we look we observe that there is a curse on the world—that it is under a moral sentence. The world groans in travail, awaiting redemption (*see* Romans 8:22).

That briefly is the content of natural revelation.

"Well, it's all pretty foggy, fuzzy, and hard to understand," you might be tempted to say. You may misread Romans 1:20 as saying that the invisible things of Him from the creation are fuzzy. But the words of Scripture are not "fuzzy" but "clearly seen." Natural revelation is clear. No one can beg off because of ignorance. There is no alibi for atheism and there is no excuse for agnosticism.

Results of Rejection. But if creation is so evidently the work of the Creator, why have men missed that conclusion? The difficulty is not in revelation but in man. Romans 1:21–23 tells us:

> Because that, when they knew God, they glorified him not as God, neither were thankful; but became vain

in their imaginations, and their foolish heart was dark-
ened . . . . They . . . changed the glory of the uncor-
ruptible God into an image made like to corruptible
man, and to birds, and four-footed beasts, and creeping
things.

When man deliberately rejected the truth that may be
known about God through nature, God gave him up to idolatry
(*see* Romans 1:23), to sexual impurity (*see* verses 24–27), and
to a reprobate mind (*see* verse 28). And now man can't know
God anymore despite living in a world that shows God's
character, attributes, power, and works.

That situation persists today. Spiritually, man is dead (*see*
Ephesians 2:1). A dead man doesn't respond. Man is blind (*see*
Ephesians 4:18). A blind man can't see the truth no matter
how well it is illuminated. The same verse tells us that not
only is unregenerate man dead and blind but he is also ignorant. Dead. Blind. Ignorant. What a terrible result of sin!

The Light Inside.   Natural revelation is not confined to creation alone. That is external. Natural revelation also comes via
conscience. That is internal. Romans 1:19 declares, "That
which may be known of God is manifest in them . . . ." Men
today, because of what they have on the inside, are conscious
that God is. Even Albert Einstein felt he had to believe in a
cosmic power. He was convinced that a man who did not
believe in a cosmic power as the source of all things was a fool.

Now a person can deny that, of course. The Bible says that
the fool says in his heart, "There is no God" (Psalms 14:1).
Interestingly enough, the word *fool* can also be translated
"wicked." Atheists are wicked. That is how they get to be
atheists. They have wickedly reduced God to nonexistence in
order to entertain their sins without a sense of moral obliga-
tion.

In order for the fool to say the word *God*, however, he has to
have a concept of God. And if he has a concept of God, that
implies that God is. It is impossible to think of something that

is not. Therefore, he is trying to eliminate something that his very reasoning powers tell him must exist. For the fool to work hard enough to eliminate God is testimony that God must be or the fool wouldn't have to worry about getting rid of Him.

Nature, then, is God's self-disclosure in man and around man. Herschel, the astronomer, said, "The broader the field of science grows, the more manifold and irrefutable become the proofs for the eternal existence of a creative and omnipotent wisdom." Linnaeus, the one-time professor of medicine and botany at Uppsala, declared, "I have seen the footsteps of God." Kepler, the astronomer, testified, "In creation I grasped God as if he were in my hands."

A Christian leader of the third century, widely known for his wisdom, was once asked where he got such wisdom.

> The source of all I have learned is in two books. The one is outwardly small, the other is very large. The former has many pages, the latter only two. The pages of the former are white with many black letters on them. One of the pages of the big book is blue, and the other is green. On the blue page there is one big golden letter and many small silver ones. On the green page there are innumerable colored letters in red, white, yellow, blue, and gold. The small book is the Bible; the large one is nature.
>
> These two books belong together. Both testify to the revelation of the one living God; their testimonies are in harmony and point to the power, greatness, and love of the Lord of the world.

So we have natural revelation given to man both by way of creation and by way of conscience. But there is something strange about the efficacy of natural revelation to save an individual. The only place and time that natural revelation was sufficient was before the Fall of Man in the Garden of Eden. Back then, there was no sin. There was no barrier. Adam and Eve could live with God out of the depths of pure hearts. God didn't need to write anything down in the garden. But after the Fall, natural revelation was not enough. The barrier could be broken only by the coming of the Lord Jesus Christ. So God wrote to tell of His coming (the Old Testament) and recorded what happened when He came (the New Testament).

The New Testament makes this clear. Jesus said, "I am the way, the truth, and the life: no man cometh unto the Father, but by me" (John 14:6). Peter said, "Neither is there salvation in any other: for there is none other name under heaven given among men, whereby we must be saved" (Acts 4:12). Jesus told men that they were condemned because they did not believe on Him (*see* John 3:18). Paul declared in Acts 16:30, 31 that faith in Christ is necessary.

Special Revelation. God has given us something beyond natural revelation. It takes up where creation and conscience leave off. We call it special revelation. Special revelation tells us all we need to know about God—information that was never before understood. It tells us about God's mercy—about His grace—about the forgiveness of sin. It tells about the sacrifice of Christ—about salvation—about the church.

Special revelation gives us specifics, not merely generalities as natural revelation does. When God speaks He doesn't mumble. God talks pointedly, exactly, even to the very simplest choice of words, to the selection of the proper cases, the verb tenses, even to the difference between plurals and singulars.

God's special revelation came progressively—by slow and gradual steps. When you read the Book of Genesis, do you get all the revelation of God? No, it is very limited. If you read only the Old Testament, would you get all the revelation of God? No, it, too, is limited. It is not wrong, it is merely progressive. The Scripture is progressing revelation in the sense that it goes from incompleteness to completeness (not from truth to error).

Do you know that some of the Old Testament prophets, according to 1 Peter 1:10–12, used to look at what they wrote and try to figure out what it meant? They would search in their own prophecies to determine the fulfillment regarding the Messiah.

So, special revelation was a process. First God revealed Himself in just a small frame, then in larger measures. First it was to a man, then to a family, then to a tribe, then to a nation, then to a race, and ultimately to the world.

God in Human Form. Now how has God revealed Himself in special revelation? In three main ways. The first is theophany—the visible appearance of God in some form. God at times in the Old Testament appeared as a man, as on the occasion in Genesis 18 when Abraham had some visitors— God and two angels. Abraham said, in effect, "Hello. You guests come into my house. Sarah, get in that kitchen and whip up something." Imagine it—Abraham and his wife fixing a proper meal to entertain God and two angels! In this case, God assumed human form to make an appearance.

There were many other ways God revealed Himself in physical form. Exodus 3 gives the account of Moses and the burning bush. God appeared as the Shekinah Glory in the Tabernacle (*see* Exodus 33–40). In Genesis 32 we have the account of Jacob wrestling with an angel—God. Theologians call this a Christophany—a preincarnate appearance of Christ.

The greatest theophany of all, of course, concerns the coming of the Lord Jesus Christ in human form to walk on earth and to dwell with men. God is not a man, as the Bible clearly teaches. "God is a Spirit" (John 4:24). But God has chosen to reveal Himself in human form, and that most perfectly in Christ.

Note that in each of these cases, God's special revelation accomplished specific purposes. God said specific things to Abraham, to Moses, and to the others. They had no doubt about what God was trying to communicate to them.

A Second Way. Every time God wanted to communicate specifics, however, it was not necessary for Him to appear in person. He could speak through the mouth of a prophet. The man of God would open his mouth and say, "Thus saith the Lord." God would take control of his mind and mouth. In fact, sometimes in studying the prophets it is impossible to tell whether it is God or one of the prophets speaking.

Take Deuteronomy 18:18, for example: "I will raise them up a Prophet from among their brethren, like unto thee, and will put my words in his mouth; and he shall speak unto them all that I shall command him." Here is a prophecy concerning Christ, but it is also a picture of a human prophet.

The commission of Jeremiah as a prophet is another example: "Then the Lord put forth his hand, and touched my mouth. And the Lord said unto me, Behold, I have put my words in thy mouth" (Jeremiah 1:9). So when Jeremiah opened his mouth, God's Word came out.

Count the Ways.   It is also amazing to notice how God got His messages across in addition to prophecy. Sometimes He communicated by the casting of lots, as in Jonah chapter 1. God wanted Jonah to take a short ride in a long fish and God wanted to make sure it would happen that way. So the pagan sailors on board the sinking ship cast lots, and the lot fell on Jonah. God made sure Jonah got the short stick. In Leviticus 16 and Numbers 26 God even gave instructions about the casting of lots.

Another fascinating way God communicated to His people was through use of the Urim and the Thummim. Leviticus 8:8 and Numbers 27:21 mention their function, although no one today is quite clear as to their exact identification. All we know is that they were something to fit into the breastplate of the high priest—perhaps two beautiful stones or jewelry. Somehow they were used to tell the will of God.

God also communicated through dreams, especially in Genesis 28, 37, 40, and 41. Another very common way for God to communicate was through visions. Daniel had both dreams and visions to learn the will and purposes of God.

At times God communicated by speaking audibly. For example, God said to Abraham, "Get thee out of thy country, and from thy kindred, and from thy father's house, unto a land that I will shew thee" (Genesis 12:1).

Think of the Apostle Paul on his way to Damascus. All of a sudden the Lord talked to him right out of heaven. What a fantastic concept. God could send His voice across the sky, from wherever heaven is, to communicate verbally.

The Means of a Miracle. A third major way God communicated in addition to nature and prophecy was through miracles. A miracle simply defined is God interjecting Himself into the laws of nature to disrupt them that He may specially reveal Himself.

Jesus verified His teaching by the divine intervention of miracles that people might know God was being revealed. The entire Gospel of John supports this. Mark 2 gives a good illustration of how God revealed Himself through miracles. Jesus healed the lame man as easily as He could forgive the man's sins. This miracle demonstrated and authenticated the deity of Christ.

God used miracles to attest to the truth of His preaching. Elijah, for example, would come and start announcing what God had said, and everyone would say, "Ha! How do we know you're telling the truth?" Then Elijah would raise somebody from the dead. Everyone would then agree, "Well, maybe this fellow is right."

Peter stands up and preaches the Gospel. Then he heals the sick. That makes people wake up and say, "This man must really be from God."

You see, God, in the New Testament especially, accompanied His Word with signs in order that men might know that it was His Word. In 2 Corinthians 12:12 Paul talks about signs and wonders and mighty deeds of the apostles that are used to certify the Word.

God Is. Any miracle testifies that God exists. It is one way God lets us know, "I am here, and I have something to say."

We should note that it is no problem for God to perform a

miracle. He made the world, didn't He? For God, a miracle is just like sticking His finger into a pond and making waves. And when God does a miracle, it doesn't go bouncing through nature and create havoc for all the rest of time until Jesus comes. It is self-contained. For example, Jesus stood at the tomb and said, "Lazarus, come forth" (John 11:43), and Lazarus came out and took off the grave clothes. But later he died again.

Ernest Renan, in his book *The Life of Jesus,* regarded Bible miracles as legends. For example, he explained the raising of Lazarus this way: it was pure hypothesis. Lazarus was only spoken of as if he really had been raised from the dead. Renan further called it a tradition: "When we know out of what inaccuracies, what incoherent fables, the gossip of an Eastern city is made up, we cannot regard it as impossible that a rumor of this kind was spread abroad." At times we are led to infer that the family of Bethany was guilty of some indiscretion, or fell into an excess of zeal.

Apparently Renan was saying that the family wanted people to really believe in the power of Christ, so Lazarus faked being dead and set up a phony resurrection. He may have had himself placed in the tomb and then had Mary and Martha put on an act.

For All to See.   Miracles do stand—and so do all the other means through which God has chosen to reveal Himself. And they are recorded for us in the Bible, the embodiment of God's self-disclosure.

Jesus never healed anyone, Renan said. He only aided people who were sick by His gentleness so that they felt better. But His followers considered these actions miracles. At the Sea of Galilee, according to Renan, Jesus was not walking on water but was stepping on a very heavy growth of lily pads.

How did the feeding of the five thousand occur? Renan declared that a large quantity of food was stored in a nearby cave. Jesus knew about it and ordered His disciples to sneak it out. All the people then thought they had witnessed a miracle.

All this is simply a denial of biblical authority. It takes more faith to believe those explanations than it does to accept the Bible record just as it stands.

Isaiah, in his day, even with all God said in the Old Testament, wanted more: "Verily thou art a God that hidest thyself . . . . Oh that thou wouldest rend the heavens, that thou wouldest come down . . ." (Isaiah 45:15; 64:1).

And He did:

> God, who at sundry times and in divers manners spake in time past unto the fathers by the prophets, Hath in these last days spoken unto us by his Son, whom he hath appointed heir of all things, by whom also he made the worlds; Who being the brightness of his glory, and the express image of his person, and upholding all things by the word of his power, when he had by himself purged our sins, sat down on the right hand of the Majesty on high.
>
> Hebrews 1:1–3

This becomes clear in the next aspect of our study.

3

God Has Spoken—
But by What Method?

Revelation and inspiration are not the same. Revelation is the message and inspiration is the method of delivering it. Revelation is God's revealing of Himself and His will. Revelation is God's self-disclosure. Inspiration is the way in which He did it. Inspiration is the act of the Holy Spirit in taking revelation and putting it through human writers who wrote the Old and New Testaments in order to set down in exact and authoritative words the message that God wanted delivered.

In order to make our definition clear, let us look at what inspiration is not. First, *inspiration is not a high level of human achievement.* Think of Homer's *Odyssey,* Mohammed's Koran, Dante's *Divine Comedy,* or Shakespeare's tragedies. Some people say that the Bible is inspired in the same way that those great works of literature were inspired. In other words, the Bible, they say, is just the product of genius—it is natural inspiration. Therefore, the Bible has errors and mistakes in it, fallible material that we can't believe. Oh, sure, they tell us, the Bible has high ethics and morals in certain parts and great insights into humanity, but it is, after all, only an achievement on the same level as other great writings.

But we have problems with that view—and we should. It says that God didn't write this Book—smart men did. But would smart men write a book that condemns men to hell? Would smart men write a book that provides no human means

of salvation apart from the perfect sacrifice of Jesus Christ?
No! Man writes books that exalt himself. He doesn't write
books to damn himself. The Bible is not simply the product of
human achievement.

How Far? Second, *inspiration is not extended just to the
thoughts of the writers.* Some say that God never gave the
writers specific words but only general ideas that they put
down in their own choice of vocabulary. It is as if God zapped
Paul with a thought about what a nice thing love is, and then
the apostle sat down and wrote 1 Corinthians 13: "Though I
speak with the tongues of men . . ." (verse 1). Men were left
free to say what they wanted to say. And that is why, though
the overall truths are divine, many mistakes appear in the
Bible, according to this belief.

But that view doesn't square with what the Bible teaches.
Paul said in 1 Corinthians 2:13, "We speak, not in the words
which man's wisdom teacheth, but which the Holy Ghost
teacheth . . . ." The "words" are the words of the Spirit, Paul
declared. Inspiration lay not just in concepts, not just in
thoughts, but in the very words.

Jesus said, "I have given unto them the words which thou
gavest me . . ." (John 17:8). Some 3,808 times in the Old
Testament we have expressions such as, "Thus saith the
Lord," "The Word of the Lord," and "The Word of God."
These phrases could hardly express wordless concepts. God
communicates in words.

Take the case of Moses. When Moses tried to excuse himself
from God's call on the basis of a speech problem, God didn't
say, "I will inspire your thoughts." He did promise, "I will be
with thy mouth . . . and will teach you what ye shall do"
(Exodus 4:15). God didn't inspire thoughts. He gave words.

That is why, forty years later, Moses was so insistent on
giving verbatim instructions to the people of Israel: "Ye shall
not add unto the word which I command you, neither shall ye
diminish ought from it, that ye may keep the commandments
of the Lord your God which I command you" (Deuteronomy

4:2). Don't add to the word and don't take away from the word. Why? Because God gave me these specific words for you, Moses was saying.

From the Holy Spirit. One of the greatest arguments against "thought inspiration" is found in 1 Peter. It alludes to the work of the prophets in the Old Testament in telling of salvation:

Of which salvation the prophets have enquired and searched diligently, who prophesied of the grace that should come unto you: Searching what, or what manner of time the Spirit of Christ which was in them did signify, when it testified beforehand the sufferings of Christ, and the glory that should follow.

1 Peter 1:10, 11

The Spirit gave the writers prophecies. The men wrote them down, read them, and then tried to figure out what they meant.

"Well," you say, "what's so amazing about that?"

It is the fact that they received words without understanding. They recorded what they were told, but they didn't understand what they were writing in its full implication. God didn't give them thoughts that they then expressed in their own words. God gave them the very words. That is why we make such an important point out of pronouns, prepositions, and even small conjunctions—all kinds of things in Scripture that seem minimal. Jesus said in Matthew 24:35, "Heaven and earth shall pass away, but my words shall not pass away."

The exchange between Peter and Christ supports the word-inspiration idea. When Peter said, "Thou art the Christ, the Son of the living God," Jesus answered, "Flesh and blood hath not revealed it unto thee, but my Father which is in heaven" (Matthew 16:16, 17). Peter was speaking right off the top of his head what God was planting in his brain. God gave him specific words, not just thoughts.

One writer has said, "Thoughts are wedded to words as soul

to body." As far as thoughts being inspired apart from the words which give them expression, you might as well talk about a tune without notes or a sum without figures. We cannot have geology without rocks, or anthropology without men. We cannot have a melody without music, nor can we have a divine record of God without words. Thoughts are carried by words, and God revealed His thoughts in words.

So inspiration is not merely extended to thoughts. It extends to the very words. We call that verbal inspiration.

Goose-Bump Theology.   Now there is a third thing that inspiration is not. *Inspiration is not the act of God on the reader.* There are some who teach what I call existential inspiration, which means that the only part of the Bible that is inspired is what zaps you. You read along and you get sort of an ethical "goose bump." At that point, the word is inspired *to you.* It is the Bible when it hits you. If you get ecstatic and emotional, convicted or confronted, then it is God's Word to you. But if you just sit there unresponsively, then it is not the Word of God. It is not authoritative.

Goose-bump theology will never do. Those who hold it also say there are myths in Scripture and so "demythologize" the Bible. They get rid of what they think is untrue. So they may edit out the preexistence of Christ, the Virgin Birth, the deity of Christ, the miracles, the substitutionary death, the Lord's Resurrection, His ascension, His return, and His coming judgment. All of that, they maintain, is historically false.

But to reject the historical character of Scripture and maintain that it can still say something—that doesn't make sense. If the Bible lies from beginning to end historically, why should we believe it spiritually? If the Book is lying where it is verifiable in history, why should we believe it in its spiritual content where we can't verify it? It seems to me that if God wanted us to trust the spiritual character of the Bible, then He would make sure that the historical and verifiable character of the Bible would substantiate its truth.

Jesus said in John 17:17, "Thy word is truth." Truth. Inspiration is not the inspiration of the reader.

Personality in the Bible. There is a fourth and final thing that inspiration is not. *Inspiration is not mechanical dictation.* The Bible writers were not robots, moving their arms in a semicomatose sort of way, just cranking it all out. The people involved were not merely secretaries and stenographers with no minds of their own involved.

It is true that God could have used dictation to give us the truth without any kind of corruption. He didn't have to use men. God could have spoken His Word into existence and then dropped it down on us like revelatory rain.

But we know that He didn't do it that way because when we open the Bible we find personality. Every book has a different character. Each author has a unique style. There are variations in language and vocabulary. And when we read the various books of the Bible, we can feel the emotions the writers were experiencing at the time.

At Work in the Man. But how could the Bible be the Word of God and at the same time, for example, the words of Paul? The answer is, because God formed the personality of the writer. God made Paul into the man He wanted him to be. God controlled his heredity and his environment. When a man had reached the point that God desired and intended, then God directed and controlled the free and willing choice of the man so that he wrote down the very words of God. God literally selected the words out of the man's own life, out of the man's own personality, his own vocabulary, his own emotions. While the words were man's words, in reality his own life had been so framed by God that they were God's words as well. So we can as easily say that Paul wrote Romans as we can say God wrote it and be correct in both statements.

David testified in 2 Samuel 23:2, "The Spirit of the Lord spake by me, and his word was in my tongue." He says it was him and it was by his tongue, but it came out as God's Word.

Fantastic! Holy men of God were moved along by the Holy Spirit (*see* 2 Peter 1:21). They were authors, not secretaries. They made full use of their personalities. We read Jeremiah, the weeping prophet, and we can feel him weeping. We read about the roaring, raging fire burning inside Amos, and we can experience it. Personality comes through every part of Scripture.

So we may define inspiration in a negative way by stating what it is not. Inspiration is not a high level of human achievement. Inspiration is not confined to thoughts alone. Inspiration is not the act of God on the reader. And finally, inspiration is not mechanical dictation.

To comprehend what inspiration is, we need to look at two passages. In 2 Timothy 3:16 we read, "All scripture is given by inspiration of God . . . ." That could be translated, "All scripture is God breathed" because the Greek word *thĕŏpnĕustŏs* comes from the words *God* and *breath*.

But what is meant by that expression? It means that which comes out of God's mouth—His Word. And as we study the matter we discover that this is the method by which God has acted. Earlier we considered the matter of natural revelation. How did that come about? By the breath of God: "By the word of the Lord were the heavens made; and all the host of them by the breath of his mouth" (Psalms 33:6). God breathed the universe into existence.

Then God breathed the Bible into existence. Special revelation comes about in the same way natural revelation did—by the breath of God. Whatever the Scriptures say, God said. In fact, the Bible personifies Scripture as God speaking. For example, Paul wrote, "The *Scriptures say*, In thee shall all the nations be blessed" (*see* Galatians 3:8). And in Galatians 3:22, "But the *scripture hath concluded* all under sin, that the promise by faith of Jesus Christ might be given to them that believe" (author's italics). Here the Bible speaks and acts as the voice of God.

We find the same thing in the Old Testament. In Exodus God said to Pharaoh, "And in very deed for this cause have I raised thee up, for to shew in thee my power; and that my name may be declared throughout all the earth" (Exodus 9:16). That is God speaking. Paul refers to this conversation in Romans 9:17, but he changes one part: "For the *scripture saith* unto Pharaoh, Even for this same purpose have I raised thee up . . ." (author's italics). When the Scripture speaks, God speaks. When God speaks, the Scripture speaks. In every sense, when you pick up the Word and read it, you are hearing God's voice. That is exciting. God is the author of what Scripture records. The Bible is the Word of God.

From Him Through Them to Us. The Bible writers in both the Old and New Testaments were commissioned to write the revelation of God in God's own words. Isaiah had a vision of the Lord sitting on His throne. He wrote, "I heard the voice of the Lord, saying, Whom shall I send, and who will go for us? . . ." (Isaiah 6:8). Isaiah recorded the words of God.

The Prophet Jeremiah wrote, "Then the word of the Lord came unto me, saying, Before I formed thee in the belly I knew thee; and before thou camest forth out of the womb I sanctified thee, and I ordained thee a prophet unto the nations" (Jeremiah 1:4, 5). "Then the Lord put forth his hand, and touched my mouth. And the Lord said unto me, Behold, I have put my words in thy mouth" (verse 9). What would be the results? "Because ye speak this word, behold, I will make my words in thy mouth fire, and this people wood, and it shall devour them" (5:14). That is vivid!

Ezekiel testified time after time that he spoke the words God had given him. God said to His prophet, "Son of man, all my words that I shall speak unto thee receive in thine heart, and hear with thine ears. And go, get thee to them of the captivity, unto the children of thy people, and speak unto them, and tell them, Thus saith the Lord God . . ." (Ezekiel 3:10, 11). And he did.

Paul wrote to the Galatians that it was God who gave him his message: "But when He who had set me apart, *even* from my mother's womb, and called me through His grace, was pleased to reveal His Son in me, that I might preach Him among the Gentiles, I did not immediately consult with flesh and blood" (Galatians 1:15, 16 NAS). Paul did not get his message from his fellow apostles—he got it directly from God.

Think of John the disciple. Is the Book of Revelation something he thought up? Never. "I was in the Spirit on the Lord's day, and heard behind me a great voice, as of a trumpet, Saying, . . . What thou seest, write in a book, and send it unto the seven churches . . ." (Revelation 1:10, 11).

All these Bible writers—and the others as well—gave clear-cut evidence that what they wrote was from God—that it was the breath of God. This is one essential factor of inspiration.

Some, Most, or All?   But now the question arises, "How much of Scripture is God breathed?" Let's return to 2 Timothy 3:16 and check out another of those Greek words: "All scripture is given by inspiration of God . . . ." The word *all,* in the Greek *pasa,* can be translated "every." So we may say that all Scripture and every Scripture is inspired.

Consider an analogy in the form of a statement: All ducks waddle. Does that mean that only ducks of the past waddle? No. Present ducks waddle, too. What about future ducks? Future ducks will also waddle. In other words, in whatever period of history ducks live, ducks waddle.

Here is the point: To say Scripture is God breathed means *all* Scripture, whether it has been written (Old Testament), is being written, or will be written (New Testament). Every verse is God breathed.

This unity of the Scripture was taught by the Lord Jesus when He said, ". . . scripture cannot be broken" (John 10:35). All Scripture is pure and authentic. None of it can be violated. The Lord meant all that was written, *all* that was being written, and all that would be written. All fit into the classification of holy writings of God.

In Black and White.   There is a third Greek word we need to examine—*graphe,* from which we get the term graphite—the lead that goes into a pencil. *Graphe*, then, is just writing. All writing—all Scripture. Note 2 Timothy 3:15: "And how from childhood you have been acquainted with the sacred writings which are able to instruct you for salvation through faith in Christ Jesus" (RSV). When we talk about writing being inspired, we refer to the Scriptures only—the "sacred writings."

There is a point here that we might miss. What is it that is inspired? The writers? No, the writings. Paul was not inspired, but the Book of Romans that he wrote was inspired. And that is true of the other letters that he wrote. They were inspired, but not the author. "All *Scripture*," said Paul.

The Bible never says that Moses was inspired, or David, or Paul—not the men but the message. That is why a man could write an inspired message at one period in his life but no other during the remainder of his life. It was the message that was inspired, not the man. The only writing that is inspired of God is the holy writing, as 2 Timothy 3:15 points out.

Despite that teaching, however, we have people around today who want to remove this verse, that verse, and some other verse or passage from Scripture. They decide what goes in and what stays out. The principle they follow is something they call the "spirit of Jesus." Whatever in the Bible fits the spirit of Jesus, they accept. Whatever doesn't fit the spirit of Jesus, they reject.

Perhaps they are reading in the New Testament and come across our Lord's cleansing of the Temple. These liberals will deny that this incident took place, or that it is really a part of Scripture because it isn't in the spirit of Jesus. Their conception of Jesus is a sort of Casper Milquetoast character who is so meek and gentle that He has no sense of judgment or justice. They make Jesus out to be just what they wish, and they throw out of Scripture anything that doesn't conform to their preconceived idea of their "fantasy Jesus."

But listen to what Jesus says: "For truly I say to you, until heaven and earth pass away, not the smallest letter or stroke shall pass away from the Law, until all is accomplished" (Matthew 5:18 NAS). The Greek words refer to a very small mark, similar in size to our punctuation marks, stuck under a word like a dot or a comma. But not one shall be removed. It is not to be touched—it is just that serious. Yet we have people going through the Bible cutting out whole passages.

Warnings in the Word.   Jesus warns, "Whoever then relaxes one of the least of these commandments and teaches men so, shall be called least in the kingdom of heaven . . ." (Matthew 5:19 RSV). God doesn't want anyone tampering with His words.

What would it take to change the Word of God? The Lord told us in Luke 16:17: "But it is easier for heaven and earth to pass away than for one stroke of a letter of the Law to fail" (NAS). It is easier for the entire universe to fold up than for the smallest mark in the Bible to be altered. God's Word is eternal!

That doesn't mean that men can't or won't tamper with it. Jesus told the Pharisees that they had invalidated the Word of God by their tradition which they had handed down (*see* Mark 7:13; Matthew 15:1–9). They had destroyed the effectiveness of Scripture by their additions and misinterpretations. In setting aside a part, they were in effect casting aside the whole, for the Bible is a unit that cannot be broken.

> Thy word is true from the beginning: and every one of thy righteous judgments endureth for ever.
>
> Psalms 119:160

Prophecy From the Holy Spirit.   There is another important passage that bears on this matter: "But know this first of all, that no prophecy of Scripture is a *matter* of one's own interpretation, for no prophecy was ever made by an act of human will, but men moved by the Holy Spirit spoke from God" (2 Peter 1:20, 21 NAS). That refers to origin. Scripture did not originate privately. It didn't come out of a man's mind.

Then how did it come? By men being carried along by the Holy Spirit.

"But this is talking only about prophecy," you point out.

Yes, but prophecy isn't just prediction. Genesis, Exodus, Leviticus, Numbers, and Deuteronomy are prophecies. The writer of those books, which we call the Pentateuch, was Moses, and Moses was a prophet.

There are some predictions as to the coming Messiah, but basically those books are history. But again, prophecy doesn't have to be predictive. Prophecy means speaking forth, a telling forth. A prophecy is a communication from God, and all communication from God came not by the will of man but by men used as they were borne along by the Holy Spirit. That is how inspiration worked.

We can sum up our look at inspiration so far by defining it as God's revelation communicated to us through writers who used their own minds and their own words. Yet God had so arranged their lives and their thoughts and their vocabularies that the words they chose out of their own minds were the very words and only the very words that God determined from eternity past they would use to write His truth.

"That's a miracle!" you exclaim.

Correct! And if you want a title for it, theologians have called it the plenary verbal inspiration of Scripture. Plenary means all. So all the God-breathed Word is in the Scripture. Nothing is missing. Verbal means word. So every word in the Bible is God breathed. Nothing in it is uninspired.

No Mistakes. Now what logically follows from that definition? At least six things. The first is that the Bible is *infallible.* If God wrote it, it has to be. Psalms 19:7 says, "The law of the Lord is perfect . . . ." It is absolute perfection just as it stands. It doesn't need anything added or taken away.

In addition to being perfect, the Bible is also *inerrant* in the original manuscripts—no mistakes. It is true that as the Bible has come down to us through the generations of man, scribes have made little changes here and there and manuscripts may have slight variations. These are obvious and known to us. But basically, as it stands today, we can look at the totality of the Word of God and say, "This is, as it stands in the original language, the Word of God Himself." Even as He upholds the world by the word of His power, so he upholds the Bible in an infallible state.

That should caution us again about tampering with the Word of God. And if we don't get the message, the Bible warns us, "Do not add to His words Lest He reprove you, and you be proved a liar" (Proverbs 30:6 NAS). When anyone comes along and wants to add a new revelation or a new inspiration, he falls into the category of those described in Revelation 22:

> I warn every one who hears the words of the prophecy of this book: if any one adds to them, God will add to him the plagues described in this book, and if any one takes away from the words of the book of this prophecy, God will take away his share in the tree of life and in the holy city, which are described in this book.

Verses 18, 19 RSV

No More Needed. What else is Scripture beyond infallible and inerrant? It is also *complete*. The Bible is all that we need. We don't need a vision. We don't need a new revelation. We need not listen for a voice from heaven. The Scriptures are complete as given. It is the ". . . faith which was once for all delivered to the saints" (Jude 3 RSV).

Our New Testament books demanded for their authentication authorship by an apostle or someone close to an apostle. Ephesians 2:20 tells us that the apostles were the foundation of the church. In this twentieth century the foundation is not being relaid. There are no more apostles; therefore, there are no more revelations. Today we enjoy the illumination of Scripture by the Holy Spirit, not by contemporary inspiration.

The Word of God is also *authoritative*. When it speaks, we had better respond. "Hear, O heavens, and give ear, O earth; for the LORD has spoken" (Isaiah 1:2 RSV). That says it all. This is God's voice recorded in Scripture, and we'd better hear it.

Then fifth, the Bible is *sufficient.* Because the Word of God is the breath of God, we don't need anything else. Go back again to that basic text, "All Scripture is inspired by God and profitable for teaching, for reproof, for correction, for training in righteousness; that the man of God may be adequate, equipped for every good work" (2 Timothy 3:16, 17 NAS). The King James Version says, ". . . That the man of God may be perfect . . . ." Is there anything needed beyond perfection? Is there anything missing? That is what we mean when we say the Bible is sufficient. Paul wrote to Timothy that "from childhood you have known the sacred writings which are able to give you the wisdom that leads to salvation through faith which is in Christ Jesus" (2 Timothy 3:15 NAS). The Bible is all he needs to find salvation and to become perfect or mature.

When a person comes along to trouble you and says, "Oh, you need this spiritual or mystical experience," don't believe it. You don't need it. All you require is the Word. The Spirit of God acting through the Word of God is sufficient to make you fully mature in Christ.

Now we have said that the Bible is infallible, inerrant, complete, authoritative, and sufficient. One thing more: The Bible is *effective.* "For the word of God is living and active and sharper than any two-edged sword, and piercing as far as the division of soul and spirit, of both joints and marrow, and able to judge the thoughts and intentions of the heart" (Hebrews 4:12 NAS). God said, "So shall My Word be which goes forth from My mouth; It shall not return to Me empty, Without accomplishing what I desire, And without succeeding *in the matter* for which I sent it" (Isaiah 55:11 NAS). And Paul said to the Thessalonians, "For our gospel did not come to you in word only, but also in power and in the Holy Spirit and with full conviction . . ." (1 Thessalonians 1:5 NAS).

The Word of God is effective—I have experienced this in my life. The Bible is a powerful book. It tears me up and it puts me back together again. Take the Word of God and the Spirit of God and you've got dynamite.

One of the reasons I know that God wrote the Bible is that it tells me things about myself that only He and I know, and usually at a depth I never understood before. And then through the Word He rearranges me to be what He wants.

Hearing Him.   Beloved, we are to stand faithfully and carefully on this inspired Word of God which is infallible, inerrant, complete, authoritative, sufficient, and effective. But there are many people who don't. Our Lord told us why: "He that is of God heareth God's words: ye therefore hear them not, because ye are not of God" (John 8:47).

Here's the way to tell a saved person from an unsaved one: one listens to the Word of God and the other doesn't. Are you listening?

4

What the Bible Says
About Itself

Imagine that you are in a court of law and that the Bible is on trial. You are counsel for the defense. What witnesses can you call to give testimony as to the veracity, the truthfulness, and the authoritative infallibility of the Bible?

I think I would appeal to at least three different sources. The first would be a group of people—the Bible writers themselves, the human instruments through which the revelation was given. Two Bible writers were kings. Two were priests. One was a physician. Two were fishermen. Two were shepherds. Paul was a Pharisee and a theologian. Daniel was a statesman. Matthew was a tax collector. Joshua was a soldier. Ezra was a scribe. Nehemiah was a butler. And on the list goes.

Writers as Witnesses. As we begin to take the testimony of these forty or more writers who wrote over a period of sixteen hundred years—ranging from Moses, who wrote the Pentateuch, to the Apostle John, who concluded with the Revelation—we discern a common note: the air of infallibility. With a few exceptions they were the simplest kind of men, without any formal education—fishermen, farmers, a tax collector, shepherds. Yet they wrote with an absolute confidence that they were setting down the Word of God.

That is astounding. Several thousand times in the Bible, in

one way or another, these men who wrote the Bible claimed to be writing the Word of God.

If I were to sit down and write something and say, "Hey folks, this is the revelation of God," people would say, "Who do you think you are?" I would be very self-conscious about making any declaration that what I had written was God's Word.

But not the Bible writers. There is no self-consciousness. There is no effort to try to convince us that they were really relating the Word of God. They just gave it, made the claim, and that settled it.

No Apologies.   You'll never find in the Bible any statement such as these: "Friends, this may sound ridiculous, but this is the Word of God." "You know, you may find this very hard to believe, but God actually gave me these words." "I know you're going to find this difficult to believe, but . . . ."

Consider Peter in Jerusalem preaching and firing off all kinds of wonderful messages. He was hauled before the Sanhedrin for trial. What did he say—"Now I realize that we are ignorant and unlearned Galileans, and you're not going to believe this, but can I speak to you from God?"

Of course not. There was an air of infallibility about his preaching, an authority in his witnessing. So he could boldly declare, "Neither is there salvation in any other: for there is none other name under heaven given among men, whereby we must be saved" (Acts 4:12).

All the Bible writers wrote with the same authority. And even though they lived in different times and circumstances, they wove a perfect, never-contradictory theme. The whole is the Word of God.

Up to Date.   These writers touched on many areas. The Bible contains history, and that history is correct. It can be verified. The Bible contains science, and that science is right, as when we read the declaration about the world: "He . . . hangeth the earth upon nothing" (Job 26:7). The Bible talks about medicine, giving laws of health as far back as Exodus. Doctors today verify that the Bible has many truths that can help produce a healthy life. The Bible talks about ethics and practical wisdom, and these have been verified as essential to a happy life.

Sometimes in the realm of science it takes man a long while to catch up with what the Bible has been saying all along. It wasn't until William Harvey's time that the discovery of the circulatory system of the human body was made. But the first book in the Bible declares that the life of the flesh is in the blood (*see* Genesis 9:4).

Herbert Spencer, who died in 1903, announced his discovery that everything in the universe fits into five categories— time, force, action, space, and matter. Everybody said, "Wonderful, Herbert, you've done it!" But Moses wrote in the first verse of the Bible, Genesis 1:1, "In the beginning [time] God [force] created [action] the heaven [space] and earth [matter]" (author's brackets).

Then there is prophecy. For example, the Bible predicted that Babylon, the greatest city of the ancient world, would be destroyed. At the time that statement was pooh-poohed as irresponsible—it was comparable to saying that the Boy Scouts were going to knock down New York. It just couldn't happen. And yet Babylon was destroyed just as the Bible said. Such examples could be multiplied.

If God didn't write the Bible, then who did? Mere men acting on their own could never have done it. The only reasonable source for such vast amounts of information was certainly outside the writers.

His Word. Now what did the Bible writers claim? Well, let's call the Old Testament authors into our courtroom and ask them. They refer to their work as being the very words of God 3,808 times. Once would be enough, but 3,808 times is more than sufficient. That amount of testimony builds a pretty substantial case.

From Psalms 19 and 119, for example, come such random statements as "The law of the Lord is perfect . . . I hope in

thy word . . . Thy word is very pure . . . Thy law is truth . . .
All thy commandments are truth . . . Every one of thy righteous judgments endureth forever . . . My tongue shall speak
of thy word: for all thy commandments are righteousness."

Amos the prophet testified, "Surely the Lord God will do
nothing, but he revealeth his secret unto his servants the
prophets" (Amos 3:7). God tells His prophets what He is going
to do. So the testimony of the Old Testament writers is that
God breathed the very words of the Book. They are infallible
and authoritative.

What about the New Testament writers? Did they believe
what the Old Testament writers believed? Well, there are at
least 320 quotations in the New Testament directly out of the
Old Testament. Check, for example, the words of Paul: "For
whatsoever things were written aforetime [the Old Tes-
tament] were written for our learning, that we through patience and comfort of the scriptures might have hope" (Romans 15:4, author's brackets). Paul considered the Old Testament writings Scripture.

Peter said that holy men of God wrote as they were borne
along by the Holy Spirit (*see* 2 Peter 1:21). Peter believed that
the Old Testament was inspired. The writer of Hebrews said
that "God, who at sundry times and in divers manners spake
in time past unto the fathers by the prophets" (Hebrews 1:1).
That writer believed the Old Testament was the Word of God.
James, in a passage describing the authority of the Old Testament writings, called them "scripture" (James 4:5).

The Witness of Acts. There are many illustrations of how
New Testament writers referred to the Old Testament, and
indicated their belief that God wrote it. Consider some in the
Book of Acts.

In his sermon Peter said, "Men and brethren, this scripture
must needs have been fulfilled, which the Holy Ghost by the
mouth of David spake before concerning Judas, which was
guide to them that took Jesus" (Acts 1:16). This is a conclusive
statement that the Old Testament was equally inspired by the

Holy Spirit. In fact, Peter was saying that the Holy Spirit used David's mouth to speak. That is a New Testament writer's view of the Old Testament inspiration.

Another example is Acts 4:25, which begins, in the King James Version, "Who by the mouth of thy servant David hast said . . . ." A better translation would be, "Who, by the Holy Spirit through the mouth of thy servant David, hast said." Here is a quotation from the Old Testament that is not only assigned to David but also to the Holy Spirit. So again, we find that the Christians in the Early Church believed that what came through David's mouth was equally the Word of God.

Those are just two illustrations from Acts underscoring the fact that the New Testament writers believed that the Old Testament words of the prophets were in fact the Word of the Holy Spirit. There are many other examples that we could cite—all written by men in the Old Testament, all spoken by men in the Old Testament, and all attributed to God in the New Testament.

One to Another. A further element concerns us. Do New Testament writers ever say that other New Testament writers are inspired? Is there any testimony from New Testament writers as to other New Testament writers? Definitely, yes.

The Book of First Timothy 5:18 sets us off on an exciting investigation: "For the scripture saith, Thou shalt not muzzle the ox that treadeth out the corn." That principle goes back to Deuteronomy 25:4. So Paul calls that Scripture. But then he adds the last part of verse 18: "And, The labourer is worthy of his reward." Now what Scripture says that? Not the Deuteronomy passage. No, we find those words in Luke 10:7 as spoken by the Lord Jesus. Paul is saying that the Old Testament in Deuteronomy 25 is Scripture, and so is the New Testament in Luke 10. So here is a New Testament writer corroborating the New Testament as Scripture.

The Book of Second Peter 3:15 and 16 provides further support. Peter says:

And account that the longsuffering of our Lord is salvation; even as our beloved brother Paul also according
to the wisdom given unto him hath written unto you; As
also in all his epistles, speaking in them of these things;
in which are some things hard to be understood, which
they that are unlearned and unstable wrest, as they do
also the other scriptures, unto their own destruction.

So Peter is saying, "I'm just telling you what our beloved
Paul said." And in doing that, Peter is declaring that all the
epistles of Paul are Scripture and do what the other Scriptures
do—instruct us in the ways of God. So what Paul wrote was as
much the Word of God as the Old Testament. Here is one of
the great statements on New Testament inspiration. It covers
Romans, 1 and 2 Corinthians, Galatians, Ephesians, Philippians, Colossians, 1 and 2 Thessalonians, 1 and 2 Timothy,
Titus, and Philemon.

The Last Word.   What about John and the Book of Revelation? At the beginning of each message to each of the seven
churches, John testifies, "These things saith he," referring to
the Lord Jesus. He also writes, in several places, ". . . let him
hear what the Spirit saith . . . ." So John is saying that all of
the Revelation is coming from Jesus Christ through him, and
that the whole is the message of the Holy Spirit. And from
place to place he drops in such expressions as "These are the
true sayings of God" (Revelation 19:9) and "These words are
true and faithful" (Revelation 21:5).

So taken all together, we have inspiration established for
the Gospels, for the epistles, and for the Book of Revelation.
So the testimony of the New Testament writers is that they
wrote the Word of God.

In addition to the testimony of the writers themselves, we
have a second witness—the Lord Jesus Christ. He had a
number of vital things to say about His view of Scripture. The
first was that He acknowledged that He was the theme of all
Scripture. In John 5:39, for example, Jesus said to the Jewish

leaders, "You search the scriptures, because you think that in them you have eternal life; and it is they that bear witness to me" (RSV).

Not only did Christ teach that He was the theme of all Scripture but He also said that He came to fulfill all Scripture. In Matthew 5:17 He said, "Think not that I am come to destroy the law, or the prophets: I am not come to destroy, but to fulfil." In Matthew 26:24 He looked at His cross and said, "The Son of man goeth as it is written of him . . . ." And a few verses later, He told Peter that He didn't need the protection of his sword, for if He wished He could call down thousands of angels for assistance. "But how then, shall the scriptures be fulfilled, that thus it must be?" (Matthew 26:54). In other words, Jesus came to fulfill Scripture. His view of Scripture was that it was all about Him and every detail had to be fulfilled.

In fact, in John 10:35, He made a staggering statement that, for me, closes the case forever: ". . . scripture cannot be broken." He meant that what God said was true and would take place. He even compared the duration of Scripture to the duration of the universe. He said, "It is easier for heaven and earth to pass, than one tittle of the law to fail" (Luke 16:17). So ". . . all things that are written by the prophets . . . shall be accomplished" (Luke 18:31).

So what was Jesus' view of Scripture? That it was the Word of God and was certain to come to pass. He even called attention to the individual words.

Psalms 22:1 predicted that when the Messiah died on the cross He would cry out, "My God, my God, why hast thou forsaken me?" Then, while dying on the cross, Jesus cried out, "My God, my God, why hast thou forsaken me?" (Matthew 27:46). Psalm 22 foretold that the suffering Saviour would thirst. On the cross Jesus cried out, "I thirst" (John 19:28).

Jesus believed in every word of the Old Testament. He corroborated the great truths of the Old Testament. For example, He confirmed the creation of Adam and Eve, in effect stating that what the Old Testament says about them is true. He said, "Have ye not read, that he which made them at the beginning made them male and female, And said, For this cause shall a man leave father and mother, and shall cleave to his wife: and they twain shall be one flesh?" (Matthew 19:4, 5). Jesus believed in the real Creation as recorded in Genesis, and He substantiated it.

Jesus and the Record.   Some have attempted to allegorize the first murder between Cain and Abel. But Jesus, in a confrontation with the Pharisees, said, "From the blood of Abel unto the blood of Zacharias, which perished between the altar and the temple: verily I say unto you, It shall be required of this generation" (Luke 11:51). Here Jesus made reference to the slaying of Abel as an actual fact.

Another thing people have denied throughout the years is the historical nature of the Flood. They don't like the idea of human sin that made it a necessity. But Jesus believed in the Noahic flood. He declared, "But as the days of Noe were, so shall also the coming of the Son of man be. For as in the days that were before the flood they were eating and drinking, marrying and giving in marriage, until the day that Noe entered into the ark" (Matthew 24:37, 38).

And there are many other facts in the Book of Genesis that He substantiated—such as the destruction of Sodom and Gomorrah and the turning of Lot's wife into a pillar of salt. In Mark 12 He affirmed the call of Moses. In John 6 He talked about the manna from heaven. In John 3 He referred to the brazen serpent lifted up in the wilderness by which Israel was healed. Over and over again, Jesus agreed to and confirmed the authority of the Old Testament record.

Jesus also established the sufficiency of the Scripture to save men. In the account of the rich man and Lazarus, the Lord quoted Abraham from the perspective of Paradise, saying, "They have Moses and the prophets; let them hear them" (Luke 16:29). The brothers of Lazarus didn't need one to rise from the dead in order for them to be saved. The testimony of the prophets was sufficient to bring them to the knowledge of the truth.

Jesus also assigned the Scriptures the ability to keep a man from error. He talked about those who erred because they didn't know the Scriptures (*see* Mark 12:24, 27).

There is an interesting statistic about the Lord's use of the Old Testament. Of the 1,800 verses of quotations of Jesus in the New Testament, 180 or one-tenth come from the Old Testament. He who is the truth, He who is the Word, knew and believed and submitted to the inspired writings of the Old Testament without reservation. If He did it, I'm willing to do it. If Jesus believed in the Old Testament, I believe in it also.

Choose One.   To sum up the testimony of Jesus about the Scriptures, we have to accept one of three possibilities. The first is that there are no errors in the Old Testament, just as Jesus taught. Or second, there are errors, but Jesus didn't know about them. Or third, there are errors, Jesus knew about them, but He covered them up.

If the second is true—that the Old Testament contains errors of which Jesus was unaware—then it follows that Jesus obviously wasn't God and we can dismiss the whole thing. If the third alternative is true—that Jesus knew about the errors but covered them up—then Jesus wasn't holy and honest.

I accept the first proposition. The Old Testament is indeed the revelation of God, inspired to give us an infallible record of God's dealing with men. Belief in the deity of Jesus Christ demands a belief in the verbal plenary inspiration of Scripture.

The Final Witness.   We have considered the witness of the Bible writers and the witness of Jesus. Now there is one more witness we must call—the Holy Spirit. The belief that the Bible is the inspired Word of God is not the result of an intellectual decision. Rather it is the result of the work of the Holy

Spirit on a person's life. An individual won't believe the Bible until the Holy Spirit has done His work of convincing him.

Let's sketch the argument. We believe the Bible is true because the Bible says it is true. But someone objects, "That's circular reasoning." Good point. If a person doesn't believe the Bible, he is not going to believe the Bible when the Bible says that it is true. On the other hand, if a person accepts the Bible as the Word of God, it is because the work of the Holy Spirit caused that truth to dawn on him.

People are not so stupid that they can't understand the truth; they are hostile so that they don't want to accept the truth. Just as Romans 1 says, men did not like to retain God in their knowledge. So when the preaching of the cross goes forth, they consider it foolishness (*see* 1 Corinthians 1:21). The natural (unregenerate) man doesn't receive the things of God (*see* 1 Corinthians 2:14). In order for his abnormal, depraved mind to receive the truth of God, the Holy Spirit must work.

So it is impossible by argument, it is impossible by preaching alone, to cause anybody to believe the Bible. Every man needs the subjective internal work of the Spirit. But the Spirit cannot produce belief in the Word of God until a person has heard the Word of God. Paul asked, "How then shall they call on him in whom they have not believed? and how shall they believe in him of whom they have not heard? and how shall they hear without a preacher?" (Romans 10:14).

Time for Decision.   Our case is finished. We have looked at the testimony of the Old Testament writers, of the New Testament writers, of the Lord Jesus Christ, and of the Holy Spirit—all defending the inspiration of the Bible. It is a very solid case. The only verdict we can possibly arrive at is yes, this is indeed the inspired Word of God that we hold in our hands.

So what are we going to do about it? We can practice Colossians 3:16: "Let the word of Christ dwell in you richly . . . ."

Our minds should be a tablet where the Word of God is written. We are to let the Bible be at home in our lives. We are to drink it in, to eat it, and to obey it. And finally, we are to pass it on.

It has been estimated that in one lifetime the average citizen will consume 150 head of cattle, 2,400 chickens, 225 lambs, 26 sheep, 310 pigs, 26 acres of grain, and 50 acres of fruits and vegetables. That's a lot of food.

But how much are we consuming of the Word of God, which gives us eternal life? An outdoor bulletin board at a church in Quincy, Massachusetts, carried this message: A BIBLE THAT IS FALLING APART USUALLY BELONGS TO SOMEONE WHO ISN'T. We have a real treasure in the Bible. May the Word of Christ dwell in each of us richly.

5

Difficulties in the Bible

Until recently the great controversy concerning the Scriptures was most frequently fought between skeptics outside the church and Christians. But now we have skeptics inside the church who espouse the heresy that the Bible contains errors. What is taught in the Bible, they say, may or may not be true. The Bible can't be trusted in every part.

This is extremely serious because the very integrity of Jesus Christ rests on the doctrine of the verbal plenary inspiration of the Bible—that the Bible is the very Word of God. We can't have a divine Saviour and an errant Bible, because Jesus said it was without error. We can't have an infallible Bible and no Saviour, because all of Scripture testifies of Christ.

Criticism Number One. There are three general areas in which the critics attack the Bible. First, they say the Bible is not inspired because it disclaims inspiration—that in some passages the Scripture denies that it is inspired.

For example, in 1 Corinthians 7 the Apostle Paul distinguishes between his instruction concerning marriage and the Lord's instruction. At first glance Paul seems to be saying that perhaps some of his writings are not inspired, as in verse 6: "But I speak this by permission, and not of commandment." Paul is saying, "I am permitting you to do something but I am not commanding you to do it." He is okaying an action but he is not ordering it.

Now what is that "something"? Being married. In verse 2

Paul says, ". . . let every man have his own wife, and let every woman have her own husband." If he stopped there, we would be in trouble because all the single people in the church would be living in open disobedience. So he says a little further down that God permits you to be married but it isn't something that you have to do.

In fact, Paul even backs off a little way from this position. He says, "I would that all men were even as I myself. But every man hath his proper gift of God, one after this manner, and another after that. I say therefore to the unmarried and widows, It is good for them if they abide even as I" (1 Corinthians 7:7, 8).

But not everyone has the gift of remaining single. So Paul adds, "If they cannot contain, let them marry: for it is better to marry than to burn" (verse 9). People may argue about what "burn" means, but I think the correct interpretation is "to burn with passion."

So Paul is saying, "When I said in verse 2 that every man may have his own wife and every woman may have her own husband, I was indicating that God allows marriage. But I am not commanding marriage, because if you are single and God has that gift for you, terrific! But if you don't have this self-control, then get married." That is practical. But is it a disclaimer to inspiration? Not at all.

Paul's Personal Opinion?   To say that Paul's writing is somehow on a lesser level of inspiration opens the door to all kinds of antibiblical practices. For example, some groups disregard Paul's teaching that women are not to usurp authority in the church and that women are not to serve as elders (*see* 1 Timothy 2:12). And so we have major denominations torn by dissension as to whether women should be ordained, and preach, and administer the ordinances.

Why don't they accept what Paul had to say? Because they think he was just giving his own personal opinion about the role of women in the church, and that Paul was old-fashioned and antifeminist in his viewpoint.

But what about the questions critics raise about 1 Corinthians 7:10 and 12? Let's see. We read in 1 Corinthians 7:10, "And unto the married I command, yet not I, but the Lord, Let not the wife depart from her husband."

Paul is stating, "I am telling you something that didn't originate with me. It originated with the Lord. I am quoting Jesus." And he goes right back to the Lord's words found in Matthew 5:31 and 32:

> It hath been said, Whosoever shall put away his wife, let him give her a writing of divorcement: But I say unto you, That whosoever shall put away his wife, saving for the cause of fornication, causeth her to commit adultery: and whosoever shall marry her that is divorced committeth adultery.

In other words, Jesus said, "Stay together!" And Paul is echoing those words. He is saying, in effect, "Now when I say to you to stay married, it's not just me saying it, but it's the Lord who commanded it."

We read in 1 Corinthians 7:12, "But to the rest speak I, not the Lord: If any brother hath a wife that believeth not, and she be pleased to dwell with him, let him not put her away." Paul is saying, "I am no longer quoting Jesus. I am speaking for myself." He is not saying that he is not inspired. Paul does not minimize his teaching; he puts it on an equal basis with the teaching of Jesus Himself.

I once knew a fellow who believed only the red letters of the New Testament. Well, I don't like red-letter Bibles because they imply that what Jesus said is more inspired and authoritative than what Paul said. But that isn't true. In the case in point, Paul was giving new, additional revelation to what the Lord had said.

So when the Bible quotes Paul as saying, "I say to you . . ." that is not minimizing Paul's opinion. That is putting his opinion on an equal basis with all Scripture, with the Old Testament, and with Christ Himself. So rather than disclaiming divine authority, he actually places his own commands on par with other Scripture teaching. Remember that as we go through the Bible we have progressive revelation.

Criticism Number Two.   Now there is a second area of criticism leveled against the Bible. The Word of God is said to be full of errors because of the process of transmission over a long period of time.

Perhaps that viewpoint could be expressed this way: "You fundamentalists may be right in saying that the original autographs of the Bible were without error, but we don't have any original autographs remaining today. You can say that what you have is the same as the original, but how do you know? Parts of the Bible were written thousands of years ago, and down through the centuries it was copied and recopied time after time. All kinds of mistakes have crept in, and we really don't know if what we have now corresponds closely to the original. The preservation and circulation of Scripture can't be guaranteed."

So what is the answer to this criticism? Well, certainly the original manuscripts were copied. This work was done by scribes, or copiers. They were specially trained and dedicated men who took on the copying process. They followed principles of checking and rechecking. Their work was long and painful, and demanded extreme care. Because they believed that they were copying the Word of God, they were extraordinarily precise. It is said that Ezra the scribe could recite *the entire Old Testament word perfect.*

Christian scholars have taken up the study of Bible manuscripts with as great an intensity. It is exciting to realize that in the opinion of most scholars today the Bible text that we hold in our hands is practically identical to the original. But is that any surprise? If God is powerful enough and intelligent enough to write the Bible, He can certainly take care of its transmission.

Do you realize that the Bible, though it is an ancient book, has been established with greater certainty than any other ancient book in existence? Thousands of Bible portions preserved on scrolls and parchments have been discovered in Bible lands. And the more that are discovered, the more we see they agree in their reading. One part is found here and the same part is found there. Place them side by side and they say the same thing. From two different cultures, from two different time periods, from two different scribes, *we have the same thing.* The fact that researchers come up with manuscripts that say the same thing is a powerful argument for their purity.

A. T. Robertson, the great scholar of Greek, counted thirteen thousand manuscript copies of the New Testament and said that all thirteen thousand essentially agree. That's exciting! God has preserved the Bible.

Textual scholars of the New Testament have noted some human errata occasioned by a scribe copying a wrong letter or vowel pointing, or perhaps inverting a word order. But these mount up to less than one word in every thousand. In fact, only one out of every 1,580 words in the Old Testament has any kind of variation from other manuscript copies.

Consider the famous Dead Sea Scrolls. You perhaps recall the story of how back in 1945 a shepherd boy was trying to chase a sheep out of a cave. He threw a rock inside and heard a piece of pottery break. So he went in and discovered many vessels holding ancient scrolls of the Old Testament, such as Isaiah.

Until 1945 Bible scholars had been basing their translations on the Masoretic text of A.D. 500. But now, with the unveiling of the Dead Sea Scrolls, they had a text going back 800 to 900 years, long before the time of Christ! And the amazing thing is that on making comparisons they found that the A.D. 500 text was the same as the B.C. text copied hundreds of years earlier. There were no substantial differences.

The Lord Jesus said that Scripture cannot be broken (*see* John 10:35). The manuscripts of the Old Testament to which Christ referred were those in the people's hands at the time. Most likely they were equivalent to the Dead Sea Scrolls. That is important because when Jesus said that the Word of

God was without error He was referring to Scripture of the same generation as the Dead Sea Scrolls. He was essentially establishing the authority of those manuscripts. There is no reasonable doubt that our present Old Testament, based on the Masoretic text of A.D. 500, and identical with the Dead Sea Scrolls used several centuries before Christ, is anything but reliable and essentially what God authored in the original autographs.

When someone comes along and says we've got transmission problems in the Bible, I say forget it. The same God who put it together originally has preserved it. If God can prepare the original writers to set down His Word without error, then God can safeguard the copiers. The manuscripts have stayed true. Jesus said, ". . . my words shall not pass away" (Matthew 24:35).

Criticism Number Three.   In addition to possible disclaimers of inspiration, and in addition to the transmission question, there is a third area in which critics attack the Bible. They contend that there are errors in the Bible that cannot be reconciled.

There are no errors in the Bible, but there are difficulties masquerading as errors. Parts of the Scripture are difficult to harmonize. However, difficulties disprove collusion on the part of writers. If the Bible were a fraud forged through collusion, it would agree with itself at every last point. The existence of difficulties is a good indication that there was no collusion.

But we do have difficulties, partly over misunderstanding the culture in which the Bible was written. Sometimes we don't understand the geography or the history of the time. We have difficulty trying to figure out what Hebrew words used thousands of years ago meant. Such difficulty is always the product of brevity and summary. When a whole historical incident is reduced to a record of five verses, for example, obviously much has been left out.

Difficulties in the Bible indicate that God's ways are higher than our ways. We can well sympathize with Peter. He wrote of Paul's letters that he found "some things hard to be understood . . ." (2 Peter 3:16). "That Paul—he's hard to understand!" Peter makes us smile, but we know exactly what he meant.

Nevertheless, let's consider several of the difficulties that critics raise and see if we can discover some answers. An old question is, Where did Cain get his wife? The answer is easy—he married his sister.

"But that's forbidden," you say.

Yes, but the prohibition came along many centuries after the time of Cain. If everybody living originally came from one family, then it is obvious that there had to be intermarriage in that first family. Genesis 5:4, 5 tells us that Adam begat many sons and daughters over his lifetime of 930 years. And Adam's sons and daughters became parents of other sons and daughters. One man has figured out that Cain could have chosen his wife from among thirty-five thousand people, so he didn't have to take the first woman who came along.

All That Glitters. Critics used to attack the Bible at the eighteenth chapter of 2 Kings, which recounts the struggle between Sennacherib, king of Assyria, and Hezekiah, king of Judah. When Sennacherib attacked, Hezekiah sought peace and said, " 'I have done wrong. Withdraw from me; whatever you impose on me I will bear.' So the king of Assyria required of Hezekiah king of Judah three hundred talents of silver and thirty talents of gold" (verse 14 NAS).

Archaeologists digging around in modern times found some interesting information about this transaction—data that apparently contradicted the Bible. They discovered that Sennacherib's official account called for eight hundred talents of silver and thirty talents of gold. That is quite a discrepancy.

Critics said, "See, the Bible is in error." They never thought Sennacherib could make a mistake, and they failed to take into consideration that they were dealing with later manuscripts rather than with the original record.

Archaeologists continued to dig in their search for more information about this famous ancient empire. More recent discoveries brought to light that while the standard for calculating gold was the same in Assyria as in Judah, the standard for figuring silver was different. They learned, in fact, that eight hundred Assyrian talents of silver were equal to three hundred Jewish talents. So once again, the Scriptures proved to be right, even to the very numbers. All that was needed was further insight and additional information.

Saved—But How? But what about the area of theology? Critics like to talk about the way Paul and James disagree. Romans 4:1–4 declares that Abraham did not get his salvation by works but by faith.

Now compare that with James 2:21: "Was not Abraham our father justified by works, when he had offered Isaac his son upon the altar?"

"There is the disagreement," the critics maintain, "an absolute contradiction. You have justification by grace and faith in Romans 4, but in James 2 you have justification by works."

But if we study this passage in question carefully, we find something very interesting. Paul is referring to Abraham in Genesis 15 while James is referring to Abraham in Genesis 22. Paul goes back to the time when Abraham was first redeemed and declared righteous. In Genesis 15 Abraham believed God and was saved by faith. But James goes back to the time when Abraham offered Isaac as a visible indication of the reality of his faith. One is saying that a man is saved by faith, the other is saying that true salvation becomes visible through good works. There is no disagreement, no contradiction at all. So once again we see that careful study on a scholarly level melts away apparent difficulties. And the Bible stands despite all of these assaults.

On the Attack.   That is defense. The Bible can defend itself. What about offense? One positive note to be sounded is the uniqueness of the Bible. There is no book like it in existence.

If we don't believe God wrote it, then we have a problem. Doctor Monier Williams, a professor of Sanskrit, spent forty years studying Eastern books, and said:

> Pile them, if you will, on the left side of your study table but place your own Holy Bible on the right side, all by itself and with a wide gap between them. For there is a gulf between it and the so-called sacred books of the east that severs the one from the other utterly, hopelessly, and forever.

Take, for example, the sacred writings of the Hindus and you find such fantastic nonsense as this:

> The moon is 50,000 leagues higher than the sun and shines by its own light. Night is caused by the sun setting behind a huge mountain several thousand feet high and located in the center of the Earth. This world is flat and triangular and is composed of seven stages: one of honey, another of sugar, a third of butter, and another of wine, and the whole mass is born on the heads of countless elephants which in shaking produce earthquakes.

Read the Koran and you find that the stars are nothing but torches in the lower heavens and that men are made out of baked clay. The grossest kinds of errors abound in Greek and Roman mythology, in the wild, disordered books of the Hindus, the traditions of the Buddhists and the Moslems. The greatest geniuses of philosophy such as Aristotle, Plato, Plutarch, Lucretius, and others wrote such absurdities that if one such absurdity were found in the Bible it would totally and forever discredit its inspiration. But there is not one such absurdity in the Bible!

One of a Kind.   The Bible is *unique.* It has been read by more people, published in more languages, studied and criticized more than any other book. God wants it circulated, and it is getting circulated. The first major book ever published was the Bible from the Gutenberg press in 1456. By 1932 the London Bible Society said there were one and a half billion Bibles in print. Nobody knows how many billion there are now.

The Bible is the only book that gives the account of special creation. It is the only book that gives a continuous historical record from the first man to the present era and on into the future. It is by far the purest religious literature with the highest moral standards. It is the only book of antiquity containing detailed prophecies of events to come. It is the only book that convicts men of sin and leads them to salvation. There is no book in the world like the Bible.

One in All. We know the Bible is true as evidenced by its uniqueness, but it is also true as seen in its *unity*. Unity in the Bible could only come from one Author guiding the whole. There are sixty-six books from forty or more human writers, ranging over sixteen hundred years from Moses who wrote the first book in the Bible to the Apostle John who was the last writer. But all are one.

One man wrote in Syria, another in Arabia, another in Italy, another in Greece. They wrote in the desert of Sinai, the wilderness of Judea, the cave of Adullam, the prison in Rome, the barren island of Patmos, the palaces of Zion and Shushan, the rivers of Babylon, and other places. We have three languages, different life-styles, different occupations, different locations, different events, poetry, history, theology, proverbs, parables, allegories, and so on, and yet there is one harmonious whole: a Mastermind controlled it all.

It is fantastic how the Bible forms a unit. Lay out the pattern of the Bible and you find four themes—revelation, history, devotion, and prophecy. In the Old Testament the first five books, the Pentateuch, constitute revelation. Then comes history, Joshua to Esther. Then comes devotion, Job to the Song of Solomon. Then comes prophecy, Isaiah to Malachi. In the New Testament, the Gospels give us history, the Book of Acts devotion, the Epistles prophecy, and the final book gives us revelation. So we have the same elements in each section of the Bible.

Consider just one theme in the Bible—salvation. In the Gospels we have salvation effected; in the Acts, salvation preached; in the Epistles, salvation explained; in the Revelation, salvation fulfilled—perfect continuity.

For Time and Eternity. Last, I think the Bible vindicates itself by its *indestructibility*. Because the Bible is God's Word, it partakes of God's nature. Since God is eternal, so is the Bible. Psalms 119:89 tells us, "For ever, O Lord, thy word is settled in heaven."

Throughout history Satan has used many means and men to attack the Bible. Diocletian, the Roman emperor, mounted the most concerted attack ever against the Bible. He killed so many Christians and burned so many manuscripts that he finally erected a column and called it *Extincto Nomine Christianorum*, which means, "The name of Christians has been extinguished." He was mistaken. Soon the Roman Empire adopted Christianity as its official religion.

The Word Goes On. Pseudoscience has tried to laugh the Bible out of existence. Centuries ago, Voltaire, the famous French writer and atheist, declared, "Fifty years from now the world will hear no more of the Bible." But in that very year, while a first edition of Voltaire's book was selling for eight cents a copy, the British Museum was paying the Russian government $500,000 for one New Testament Greek manuscript copy. And fifty years after his death the Geneva Bible Society used Voltaire's house and press to print Bibles.

Thomas Paine wrote *The Age of Reason* two hundred years ago and in it he attacked Christianity. He felt his arguments would forever destroy the Bible. He predicted that in a few years the Bible would be out of print. He boasted, "When I get through there will not be five Bibles left in America." He turned out to be off a little in his count.

It has been said that unbelievers with all their attacks on the Bible make no more impression than a man would with a toy hammer on the pyramids of Egypt.

So the hammers of infidels have been pecking away at this Book for ages, but the hammers are worn out and the anvil still endures. Praise God for His Word. What a Book. United. Unique. Indestructible.

". . . The grass withers, and the flower falls, but the word of the Lord abides for ever . . ." (1 Peter 1:24, 25 RSV).

6

Miracles in the Bible

Some people believe that miracles constitute a big problem in the Bible. If we could just get rid of the miracles they say, more people would believe it.

On the other hand, I believe that one of the greatest manifestations that the Bible is the true Word of God is the fact of miracles. In ordinary conversation we use the term loosely. We say, for example, "I was driving home last night and you'll never believe what happened. A guy went right through a red light and barely missed me. I'm telling you, it was a miracle!" Or, "I didn't have any money and unexpectedly I got a check in the mail for fifty dollars. I just praise God for this miracle!" Everything can be miraculous.

But what precisely is a miracle? Webster's Dictionary gives a poor definition, but one that fits the modern mentality. It says a miracle is "an event or effect in the physical world deviating from the known laws of nature, or transcending our knowledge of these laws." Notice that this does not say that a miracle deviates from the laws of nature but rather from the *known* laws of nature. So Webster explains miracles as a natural phenomenon, not a supernatural one.

Webster's definition of miracle does not apply to the Bible. Miracles are allowed for out of ignorance but not as something outside of and beyond the natural. The implication Webster leaves with most people is that a miracle is something that happens that can't be explained.

The Bible definition of a miracle is something quite different. In the Bible a miracle is something that happens because God intervened in the natural world and did something supernatural. By that very definition you realize that we are talking about two realms—the natural world that is here and the supernatural world that is outside.

By way of illustration, think of our world as a little box that we live in; everything in our natural box is qualified by natural law. God is outside our little box, but occasionally He pokes His finger into our box and "makes waves." God violates the natural by the supernatural.

The Bible, especially in the New Testament, describes miracles in three terms: signs, wonders, and mighty works. Miracles are mighty works to create wonders to act as signs. Now signs are not ends in themselves—they merely point to something. And miracles are not ends in themselves, but they, too, point to something. Or better, they point to Someone who is outside the box. They point to the fact that God has invaded our natural world to show that there is a supernatural world.

Two Options.   There are two responses that may be made in regard to the signs of miracles. One is the atheist's reaction. He says naturalism is all there is and that God does not exist. So consequently miracles are impossible because there is nobody outside the box. This is what the unbeliever maintains even though he has a lot of trouble explaining where the box came from in the first place.

The other response is that of the Christian. He accepts the fact that there is a spiritual, supernatural power—a source of creation outside the box. Therefore, miracles are easily allowable because the supernatural is there to act upon the natural. In fact, if there is a God, then miracles are to be expected. Otherwise we would be merely affirming that God is and then not allowing Him to do anything. If God is, then God acts because being is doing. If God is, then miracles are valid.

Anybody who believes in God *must* believe in miracles. So don't go to the Bible and say, "I'll accept this as the Word of God provided I can get rid of the miracles." That is ridiculous.

It is the same as saying, "Okay, God. You can exist. You just can't do anything."

Three Requirements. Now in order for a miracle to fit the biblical definition it has to have three qualities. First, it must be sensible. By that I mean it must be perceived by the senses. It must be something that somebody sees or hears or feels and gives testimony to.

Second, a miracle must be clear. It must be very evidently a revelation of the power and presence of God. It must transcend all natural law so that there is no other explanation for it.

And third, there must be a divine purpose to the miracle. God performs miracles to reveal to us His person. So miracles must be perceived by the senses, they must be clear, and they must have a divine purpose.

As we read through the Bible, we find that miracles in the Word of God fit all of these qualifications. The miracles recorded in Scripture are perceived by the senses of credible witnesses. They are clearly beyond any natural explanation, and they have a divine purpose of pointing toward God. While we can't examine all the Bible miracles because of space limitations, we can at least consider some of them. Let us take a look at miracles that affected all men, miracles that affected nations, and miracles that affected individuals.

Universal Miracles. The first miracle is found in the very first verse of the Bible: "In the beginning God created the heaven and the earth" (Genesis 1:1). The Bible starts out with the assumption that God is. There is no argument in the Scriptures for the existence of God. It is not a theory to be proven; it is a fact to be affirmed. The Bible never attempts to prove that God exists.

If a person declares that there is no God, the burden of proof rests on him. So when an athist says to me, "I don't believe there is a God," I reply that I believe there is a God and that the Bible affirms there is a God. He must prove to me that there is not a God, and, of course, he can't do it.

If we accept the first sentence of the Bible, we have no problem with the miracle involved. The word *created* means "to make out of nothing." If we believe God made everything out of nothing, that is a miracle. And if we allow the miracle of Genesis 1:1, then why should we be bothered by other miracles in the Bible?

The miracle of creation is certainly the greatest one in terms of volume. Can you imagine that God stepped out on the edge of nothing and made everything—by His Word alone? That is a miracle!

As we look at Genesis 1, we stand in amazement at how simply the Spirit of God describes this: "And the earth was without form, and void; and darkness was upon the face of the deep. And the Spirit of God moved upon the face of the waters" (Genesis 1:2). God created and the creation was formless. But then the creation takes form: "Let there be a firmament in the midst of the waters, and let it divide the waters from the waters. And God made the firmament, and divided the waters which were under the firmament from the waters which were above the firmament: and it was so" (verses 6, 7).

In the rest of the chapter we have a fantastically detailed and beautiful description of the Creation. Some people say, "Well, this is just a myth, just somebody's thought. This isn't how it happened."

Yet the description given in Genesis 1 contains no scientific errors at all. Not one statement has ever been proven wrong. Even the sequence of the Creation matches with what scientists have discovered. For example, if you check botany sources, you will discover that the order in which the flora and the fauna are said by the Mosaic account to have appeared upon the earth corresponds with that which the theory of evolution requires and the evidence of geology proves.

Well, Moses was no geologist. And he certainly wasn't around during the Creation to observe firsthand. But what Moses wrote is true because God gave him the revelation.

How Long a Time. But scientists stumble over the Bible statement that all of the Creation took place in six days. They reject this because they hold to the geological age system. They say that twenty billion years ago the elements and the stars and the galaxies evolved, but without explaining what they evolved from. Then five billion years ago the earth and the solar system evolved. Three billion years ago the evolution of life took place. Fifty million years ago the evolutionary ancestors of apes and men evolved. Three million years ago modern man evolved.

Scientists base their calculations on the fossil record. They find fossils in sedimentary rock, so they determine that the fossils are a certain age because they are found in that rock. Then they reverse that reasoning by saying that a rock is a certain age because of the fossils it contains. Some propound a view called theistic evolution or progressive creationism. "We believe the Genesis account," they insist, "only those weren't actual days. Those verses refer to great millions of years of passing of time." They insist that they must allow for great time periods for the strata of the earth to be formed as we now observe them.

But is that really required? The distance from my church to my home is about five miles. If I want to get to my home I could crawl. That would take me a very long time. Or I could walk all the way home in less time. Or I could get in my car and drive like a jehu. I would cover the very same ground only at different speeds.

God didn't need a lot of time for forming things if He just ran the Creation at a high speed. And that is how God did it.

If you took a leaf and laid it on a brick, it would never become a fossil by such a slow process. But if a catastrophe suddenly occurred and slammed that leaf into a rock and hermetically sealed it, then you would have a fossil. And that is how all the fossils in the sedimentary rock got there.

There is no problem if you allow for a period of time being speeded up. It is possible to take a 33⅓ record and play it back at 78 rpm. It may sound like Alvin and the Chipmunks, but it will cover exactly the same content.

I believe the Bible when it says that God created the world in six days. I think God knows how to communicate. God isn't stuck for proper grammar. He has a vocabulary that is accurate.

The Hebrew word for "day" used in Genesis is *yom*. When in the plural it always means a literal day. In six days the strata fell into place. God didn't need time and a slow pace.

The miracle of creation, then, is clear. It is sensible. How can you verify the miracle of creation? Look up. Look around you. It is obvious that someone did all of this. It is verifiable. It proves God to me. It has to prove God. Somebody had to make this! It is absurd to think that everything came from nothing.

How Did He Do It?   Let me take you to a second miracle as recorded in Genesis 6 and 7—the Flood. God told Noah to build an ark 450 feet long by 75 feet wide by 43 feet high out in the middle of a desert! "And the Lord said unto Noah, Come thou and all thy house into the ark; for thee have I seen righteous before me in this generation" (Genesis 7:1). Then God went on to give specific details about the animals that were to enter the ark.

"The whole thing is ridiculous," some people might say. "How was Noah to determine which animals should go and which must stay behind and be drowned?"

Well, it was no real problem for the God who made those animals. God has much less trouble with animals than He does with people: "The ox knoweth his owner, and the ass his master's crib: but Israel doth not know, my people doth not consider" (Isaiah 1:3). God organized the animals to do His will.

Then when the animals all went into the ark, God broke up everything: ". . . all the fountains of the great deep [were] broken up, and the windows of heaven were opened. And the rain was upon the earth forty days and forty nights" (Genesis 7:11, 12, author's brackets). A tremendous flood took place as water covered the entire earth. Mount Ararat was about 17,000 feet high, and water covered that mountain. Since water seeks its own level, that indicates a universal flood.

In the Creation and the Flood we have two great events that have given us our present world. Men explain the natural effects with theories that call for long passages of time, but Scripture states that through catastrophic means God speeded up the processes so that the Creation, which took six days, shaped the earth, and the Flood, which lasted approximately 150 days, reshaped it.

The Tower of Babel. Another miracle, recorded in Genesis 11, concerns the Tower of Babel. Men were going to build a ziggurat, a pagan tower, to worship a false god.

So the Lord did an interesting thing:

> And the Lord said, Behold, the people is one, and they have all one language; and this they begin to do: and now nothing will be restrained from them, which they have imagined to do. Go to, let us go down, and there confound their language, that they may not understand one another's speech. So the Lord scattered them abroad from thence upon the face of all the earth: and they left off to build the city. Therefore is the name of it called Babel . . . .
>
> Genesis 11:6–9

The word *babel* comes from the Hebrew word meaning "to confuse." So the Lord confounded the language of all the earth and scattered the people.

Here is a very clear and lucid and responsible explanation of where languages came from. God performed a miracle that affected all mankind.

Creation revealed God as Creator. The Flood revealed God as Saviour. Babel revealed God as Judge. All of them had the divine purpose of pointing to God.

National Miracles. Now let us look at a second category of miracles—those that have affected nations. A good example

concerns the children of Israel at the Red Sea, an account
given to us in Exodus 14.

You can imagine the situation in which Moses and the Israelites found themselves. Here they were, camped between
two mountains. Behind them came Pharaoh and the Egyptians
with all their horses and chariots. Before them lay the Red
Sea. You can understand why they would cry out to the Lord
(*see* verse 10).

"And the Lord said unto Moses, Wherefore criest thou unto
me? speak unto the children of Israel, that they go forward"
(verse 15). "Okay, Lord," Moses must have said, "but how are
we going to do it?"

> But lift thou up thy rod, and stretch out thine hand
> over the sea, and divide it: and the children of Israel
> shall go on dry ground through the midst of the sea. And
> I, behold, I will harden the hearts of the Egyptians, and
> they shall follow them: and I will get me honour upon
> Pharaoh, and upon all his host, upon his chariots, and
> upon his horsemen. And the Egyptians shall know that
> I am the Lord . . . .
>
> Verses 16–18

Now here again God is revealing Himself. He is performing
a miracle to show that He is God. Would there be any doubt
about that back in the capital of Egypt when they discovered
that their entire army had been drowned?

> And the angel of God, which went before the camp of
> Israel, removed and went behind them; and the pillar of
> the cloud went from before their face, and stood behind
> them. And it came between the camp of the Egyptians
> and the camp of Israel; and it was a cloud and darkness
> to them, but it gave light by night to these: so that the
> one came not near the other all the night.
>
> Verses 19, 20

God just plopped down His Shekinah Glory between the Egyptians and the Israelites to disturb the one and to comfort the other.

You remember what happened:

> And Moses stretched out his hand over the sea; and the Lord caused the sea to go back by a strong east wind all that night, and made the sea dry land, and the waters were divided. And the children of Israel went into the midst of the sea upon the dry ground: and the waters were a wall unto them on their right hand, and on their left. And the Egyptians pursued, and went in after them to the midst of the sea, even all Pharaoh's horses, his chariots, and his horsemen . . . . And the Lord said unto Moses, Stretch out thine hand over the sea, that the waters may come again upon the Egyptians, upon their chariots, and upon their horsemen. And Moses stretched forth his hand over the sea, and the sea returned to his strength when the morning appeared; and the Egyptians fled against it; and the Lord overthrew the Egyptians in the midst of the sea. And the waters returned, and covered the chariots, and the horsemen, and all the host of Pharaoh that came into the sea after them; there remained not so much as one of them.
>
> Verses 21–28

How Did It Happen? Now this is a miracle. There is no other logical explanation for it, although some have been offered. Some critics have said that at the north end of the Red Sea was an area called the Bitter Lakes or the Reed Sea. Between the Red Sea and the Bitter Lakes was a little marshy area two or three inches deep. A southeast wind supposedly blew up the channel and the stiffness of the wind held the water in the Bitter Lakes and the tide ebbed away in the Red Sea. And so what really happened was that the children of Israel waded through this marshy area.

That is weak—really weak. To the best of our knowledge, the Bitter Lakes and the Red Sea were fairly well separated. And even if the Israelites did march through one, two, or three inches of marshy ground, how were all the hosts of the Egyptians drowned in that place? It takes more faith to believe that explanation than it does to believe the biblical account.

Well, what did account for the strong east wind that parted the waters? The breath of God. God walled up the waters on both sides by a miracle. If we believe in God, then we should believe in this miracle. How stupid for a puny little man to stand up and say, "No, God, You couldn't have done it that way. You must not act supernaturally."

Food From Heaven. Let us consider another miracle. Exodus 16 recounts the miracle of the manna. Verses 14–22 tell us all about it. For the forty years of wandering in the desert, God provided His people with manna.

Now there are amazing explanations for this. Some explain manna as lichen, which grows on rocks and trees. The lichen was increasing in volume day after day, they say, and the people collected this and ate it as their food. But researchers believe there was no such thing in the desert of Sinai, at least there has been no trace of it in the last several hundred years.

Another suggestion is that the manna was really a sticky, light-colored, honeydew excretion that came out of tamarisk twigs. The people went along scraping this substance from the tamarisk bark.

But investigators have discovered that the substance on the tamarisk wasn't produced by the tamarisk at all but was left there by insects. And besides, the substance only appeared during the months of June and July, and it would hardly have been sufficient to feed three million people.

No, the provision of manna was a miracle. God fed His people with something that He created especially for them. And if God is God, He could do that easily enough.

One by One. In addition to miracles that have affected people and miracles that have affected nations, the Bible contains miracles that have affected individuals, such as a fascinating one in Numbers 22 concerning Balaam. Balaam was a prophet for hire, and he was doing the wrong thing:

> And God's anger was kindled because he went: and the angel of the Lord stood in the way for an adversary against him. Now he was riding upon his ass, and his two servants were with him. And the ass saw the angel of the Lord standing in the way, and his sword drawn in his hand: and the ass turned aside out of the way, and went into the field: and Balaam smote the ass, to turn her into the way.
>
> Verses 22, 23

Balaam became angry and struck his animal. He didn't see a thing, but the ass saw the angel of the Lord with a big sword. Balaam probably rode the donkey every day. But now all of a sudden the animal had gone crazy, wandering all over, and injuring the rider. No wonder Balaam was angry.

Now what follows is very interesting: "And the Lord opened the mouth of the ass, and she said unto Balaam, What have I done unto thee, that thou hast smitten me these three times?" (verse 28).

You say, "Nobody would ever believe that. No sane individual would ever believe that Balaam's ass talked!" But I can refer you to one who did—one of the most sane individuals in all the Bible, one of the most precious saints of God who ever lived. The Apostle Peter had this to say about the false teachers of his day: "Which have forsaken the right way, and are gone astray, following the way of Balaam the son of Bosor, who loved the wages of unrighteousness; But was rebuked for his iniquity: the dumb ass speaking with man's voice forbad the madness of the prophet" (2 Peter 2:15, 16). Peter believed in this miracle, and Peter was a credible witness.

Let us return to the account in Numbers 22: "Balaam said unto the ass, Because thou hast mocked me: I would there were a sword in mine hand, for now would I kill thee" (verse 29). The miracle is not that the ass spoke to Balaam—it is that Balaam answered! I think I would have fallen flat on the ground in astonishment!

Suggested Answers. What about the man who wants to believe in God but who can't believe that this miracle took place? One person said that Balaam was in a trance and mistakenly thought he heard the animal speak.

Another critic has suggested that Balaam had a habit of talking to himself. He was merely replying to himself and the witness mistook it for the talking of an animal. Yet another has said that Balaam was so used to talking to his donkey that when the donkey talked back to him, Balaam was just misinterpreting the familiar bray. They just won't admit to the possibility of a miracle.

This incident is certainly a miracle, and what astounds me is the writer's total lack of defensiveness in relating it. If I were writing this down, I would say, "Folks, I'm about to say something that you're not going to believe. There was this guy riding on his donkey, and . . . ." I would have to throw in a few little statements to prepare the readers for the jolt.

But here is something amazing about Bible writers: No matter how bizarre or how strange or how weird the miracles might seem, the writers never defend them. They only state and affirm.

Who wrote this account of Balaam and his ass? Moses, the man who was raised to the elevation of the highest place in Pharaoh's court. The man who, with his brilliant genius of leadership, led at least three million people in the wilderness. The man who was used of God to communicate revelation regarding the Ten Commandments and many other aspects of the Law. The man who wrote the Pentateuch with all its deep truths and great doctrines. The man who wrote down the sweeping history of the beginning. This man, without any self-consciousness and without one defensive statement, wrote the story about a conversation between Balaam and his donkey.

I find that exciting. It tells me God is acting. And if God is acting in this Book, then this is the kind of book I want because I want to know God.

7

The Miraculous Jesus

We have defined a miracle as an act of God by which He temporarily sets aside natural law. When God invades the natural and does something that is supernatural, we know that Somebody is active and interested in what is going on down here.

God's miracles are always purposeful. He doesn't do things in an irrational, nonsensical, haphazard way. The sort of things found in the apocryphal books between the Old and New Testaments in some Bibles are irrational. One of these "miracles," for example, says that when Jesus was a little child He would take clay and make pigeons. Then He would tap them and they would suddenly come to life and fly away. It is also recorded that one day Jesus got mad at the other children and killed them.

What nonsense. Such accounts violate all of the ethics and moral purposes we know to be true of Jesus Christ. And they violate the teaching of Scripture itself. When Jesus turned water into wine, the Scripture says, "This *beginning* of miracles did Jesus in Cana of Galilee . . ." (John 2:11, author's italics). He never performed a miracle until then.

No, miracles were never done merely to entertain people. They were done purposefully to reveal that God is and to show what God is like. They showed Him to be loving and kind and merciful, but also to be just. In the Old Testament, miracles disclosed the nature of God. In the New Testament, they revealed the deity of Christ.

Miracles prove that Jesus was none other than God Himself. Check John 5:18: "therefore the Jews sought the more to kill him, because he not only had broken the sabbath, but said also that God was his Father, making himself equal with God." They abhorred His statement that "all men should honour the Son, even as they honour the Father" (John 5:23).

Now what proof is offered that Jesus is on the same level as God? We get a clue from John 5:31 and 32: "If I bear witness of myself, my witness is not true. There is another that beareth witness of me; and I know that the witness which he witnesseth of me is true." Here Jesus is referring to John the Baptist.

There is still a further witness in verse 36: "But I have greater witness than that of John: for the works which the Father hath given me to finish, the same works that I do, bear witness of me, that the Father hath sent me."

The greater testimony to the Lord's deity is His works. If a person comes along and says, "I am God," we disregard it for lack of proof. But we believe that Jesus was God because He not only claimed to be such but He also supported it by His works. In John 10 this idea comes across clearly: "Then came the Jews round about him, and said unto him, How long dost thou make us to doubt? If thou be the Christ, tell us plainly. Jesus answered them, I told you, and ye believed not: the works that I do in my Father's name, they bear witness of me" (verses 24, 25).

New Testament Miracles.   Tremendous! The testimony that Jesus is the living Word of God is based on the miracles that He performed. As Christians we don't have to apologize or stand ashamed at the record of miracles. No, miracles give validity to the claims of Scripture to be the Word of God and to the claims of Christ to be the Son of God.

I find miracles convincing. John the Baptist did. When he was in prison John sent two of his disciples to Jesus to ask Him, ". . . Art thou he that should come? or look we for another?" (Luke 7:19). In our contemporary language, we should express it, "John wants to know if you are the Messiah that he's been announcing."

Jesus didn't launch into a long answer. Instead, "In that same hour he cured many of their infirmities and plagues, and of evil spirits; and unto many that were, blind he gave sight" (verse 21). Jesus proved that He was the Messiah by performing miracles: "Then Jesus answering said unto them, Go your way, and tell John what things ye have seen and heard; how that the blind see, the lame walk, the lepers are cleansed, the deaf hear, the dead are raised, to the poor the gospel is preached" (verse 22). They must have gasped, "Okay, okay!" And they were gone.

The convincing argument for the deity of Christ is not only His words but also His works. I believe the Bible is the Word of God because it contains miracles, and that means God is in the Book. I believe Jesus is God because He performed miracles and that means God was in Christ.

So when we come to the Bible, we come to the exciting record of a unique personality. Historian Philip Schaff wrote in his book *The Person of Christ:*

> This Jesus of Nazareth without money and arms conquered more millions than Alexander, Caesar, Mohammed and Napoleon. Without science and learning He has shed more light on things human and divine than all the philosophers and scholars combined. Without the eloquence of schools He spoke such words of life as were never spoken before or since and produced effects which lie beyond the reach of orator or poet. Without writing a single line He has set more pens in motion and furnished themes for more sermons, orations, discussions, learned volumes, works of art, and songs of praise than the whole army of great men of ancient and modern times.

Now Schaff was a believer. But even the unbelieving skeptic H. G. Wells testified in the May 1935 *Reader's Digest,* "When I was asked which single individual has left the most permanent impression on the world, the manner of the question almost carried the implication that it was Jesus of Nazareth. I agree."

The Miracle of His Birth. Everything about Jesus was miraculous. First, His birth was miraculous. The opening book of the New Testament contains the credible, responsible testimony of a man named Matthew: "Now the birth of Jesus Christ was on this wise: When as his mother Mary was espoused to Joseph, before they came together, she was found with child of the Holy Ghost" (Matthew 1:18). She was pregnant—but not by Joseph.

"Then Joseph her husband, being a just man, and not willing to make her a publick example, was minded to put her away privily" (verse 19). He had two choices: he could bring her out into the middle of the street to be stoned to death for the sin of adultery, or he could divorce her with as little fuss as possible.

Joseph assumed that a terrible tragedy had happened—Mary had had sexual relations with another man, even though they were pledged as spouses. His heart must have been broken beyond belief.

> But while he thought on these things, behold, the angel of the Lord appeared unto him in a dream, saying, Josph, thou son of David, fear not to take unto thee Mary thy wife: for that which is conceived in her is of the Holy Ghost. And she shall bring forth a son, and thou shalt call his name JESUS: for he shall save his people from their sins. Now all this was done, that it might be fulfilled which was spoken of the Lord by the prophet, saying, Behold, a virgin shall be with child, and shall bring forth a son, and they shall call his name Emmanuel, which being interpreted is, God with us.
>
> Verses 20–23

Never Before. Who was Jesus then? God with us. What a marvelous promise and fulfillment of messianic prophecies that go back to Genesis 3:15, which foretold the coming of one who would be unusually born. God said, "I will put enmity between thee and the woman, and between thy seed and her seed . . . ." But what woman ever had seed? That is the function of the man. Only once in history did woman have a seed, and that woman was Mary. The Spirit of God created it within her.

Now when ordinary humans are born, that marks the beginning of their existence. But Jesus did not begin His life at the time of His birth. That is implied in His words, "For I came down from heaven, not to do mine own will, but the will of him that sent me" (John 6:38). And the opening words of John's Gospel declare plainly, "In the beginning was the Word, and the Word was with God, and the Word was God. The same was in the beginning with God" (John 1:1, 2). The Lord has always existed. There never was a time when He was not.

Did John the Baptist know that? Check his testimony: "This was he of whom I spake, He that cometh after me is preferred before me: for he was before me" (John 1:15).

The theme of the Lord's preexistence is carried out repeatedly on the pages of this Gospel. Jesus told the Pharisees, "Your father Abraham rejoiced to see my day: and he saw it, and was glad. Then said the Jews unto him, Thou art not yet fifty years old, and hast thou seen Abraham? Jesus said unto them, Verily, verily, I say unto you, Before Abraham was, I am" (John 8:56–58). Jesus could do something with grammar that no one else can do. He could say, "I am yesterday, I am today, I am tomorrow." Only the eternal God could make such a statement.

What a marvelous birth! It was special creation. God didn't need a man to impregnate Mary. God instantly created an embryo.

"Oh," you say, "that's biologically impossible!"

Of course it is. That is why we know God did it. It was also biologically impossible to create Adam out of dirt, but God did it. And it was biologically impossible to create Eve out of the

side of Adam. But God did that, too. Biological impossibilities
are no problem for God. He is supernatural.

Held Through History.   All the historical evidence agrees
that the Early Church believed from the beginning in the
Virgin Birth. Some people say, "Oh, they just made it up."
That can't be true because the Jews never believed their Messiah would be born this way, so why would they invent something they never anticipated?

Other people say, "The Jewish Christians invented the Virgin Birth." But they never anticipated it, either. They were
shocked. Why did the Early Church believe this doctrine—
because they made it up? No, because it was true.

Let the skeptics and the doubters rail against the miraculous
birth of Christ if they will. They can't undo it. They can't
shake it. God set aside the normal requirements of two human
parents in order to bring forth His only Son, born of a virgin.

The Miracle of a Sinless Life.   This direct creative act of God
bypassed the sin problem. Whatever is born of the flesh is
flesh. Jesus was not born of the flesh but of the will of God.
And that led to the miracle of our Lord's sinless life.

What a life He lived! Hebrews 4:15 makes the amazing
statement, "For we have not an high priest which cannot be
touched with the feeling of our infirmities; but was in all
points tempted like as we are, yet without sin." Think of that:
Jesus never sinned!

Hebrews 7:26 adds, "For such an high priest became us,
who is holy, harmless, undefiled, separate from sinners, and
made higher than the heavens." That, too, speaks of His sinless life.

Even Judas with his twisted and sick mind recognized that
Jesus was sinless. He said, "I have sinned in that I have be-
trayed the innocent blood" (Matthew 27:4). This unbeliever
confessed that Jesus had never sinned.

Other unbelievers made the same judgment. Pilate said five
times, "I find no fault in him" (*see* Luke 23:4, 14; John 18:38;

19:4, 6). The thief on the cross said, "We indeed [suffer] justly; for we receive the due reward of our deeds: but this man hath done nothing amiss" (Luke 23:41, author's brackets). And the Roman centurion saw Him faultless (*see* Matthew 27:54).

It is useless to look through the entire biography of Jesus hoping to find a single stain or the slightest shadow on His moral character. Jesus could never have written Psalm 51 with its cry, "Create in me a clean heart, O God . . ." (verse 10). Jesus could never have written Romans 7, which recounts the battle between the old and new natures. Jesus could never have died, as Saint Augustine did, reciting penitential psalms. Jesus needed no forgiveness. He needed no grace. He had no sin. Jesus lived a miraculous, sinless life, the result of His supernatural birth.

Supernatural Words. A third area of the miraculous in the life of Jesus concerned His unsurpassed words. Sholem Asch was quoted by Frank S. Mead in *The Encyclopedia of Religious Quotations* as having said:

> Jesus Christ is the outstanding personality of all time . . . . No other teacher—Jewish, Christian, Buddhist, Mohammedan—is still a teacher whose teaching is such a guidepost for the world we live in. Other teachers may have something basic for an Oriental, an Arab, or an Occidental; but every act and word of Jesus has value for all of us. He became the Light of the world. Why shouldn't I, a Jew, be proud of that?

You can't read through the New Testament and not be impressed with the words of Jesus. They are startling! You recall how the Pharisees dispatched the Temple police to arrest Jesus. But they came back empty-handed, their eyes as wide as silver dollars. With their mouths hanging open they said, "Never man spake like this man" (John 7:46).

Like His birth and His sinless life, the words of Jesus were miraculous. He taught about God, angels, men, earth, heaven,

hell, past, present, and future. He posed questions no man
could answer, and He answered questions that were un-
answerable by others. Nicodemus came to Him in the night
and said, "We know that thou art a teacher come from God"
(John 3:2). How did he know it? By what Jesus had to say. His
words were supernatural.

Add His Works.   Jesus' supernatural works were another area
of the miraculous. Even as Nicodemus was impressed by the
words of Jesus, so he was impressed by His works: ". . . no
man can do these miracles that thou doest, except God be with
him" (John 3:2). Nicodemus was not at this time a believer or a
follower of Jesus. He was a teacher of Israel of the highest
ranking. It was obvious to him that God was in Christ because
of what He was doing.

The supernatural works of Christ are absolutely staggering.
The record of history shows that He performed miracles on a
nonselective basis. He healed all kinds of people of all kinds
of diseases.

Nor were the miracles of Jesus partial. He did not heal a
person of 90 percent of his trouble. There weren't any situa-
tions He could not handle. And the miracles of Jesus were
never temporary. Those He touched did not suffer relapses.

No Wine to Serve?   There are several categories into which
the miracles of our Lord fall. The first concerns His power
over nature. He would command nature, and nature would
obey. For example, He turned water into wine (*see* John 2:1–
11). Weddings were big affairs in those days. The celebration
lasted an entire week.

To serve wine was a practical necessity. To run out of wine
was a social offense. So Jesus told the servants to fill those
huge twenty- or thirty-gallon water pots. And when they had
done so, He ordered, "Take some out to the steward." And
they did.

The steward tasted the water that had been turned into wine
and said, "This is unusual! Ordinarily at the end of the wed-

ding you get the inferior wine, when you are insensitive and can't taste it too well. But this is the greatest I've ever had!"

Isn't it amazing that apparently no fanfare was associated with this first miracle of Christ? There is no record that the angels sang or heaven shook or the earth rattled. Jesus did not climb on the roof and shout out over the assembly, "Wine!"

I think Jesus probably just looked at those stone water pots and that was it. For the One who created the universe, a few gallons of wine was a small thing. There were plenty of witnesses who corroborated this miracle. And John recorded it in the second chapter of his Gospel.

Nothing for Dinner?   One day Jesus stood on the side of a hill at the Sea of Galilee, and there were probably twenty thousand people gathered around Him—five thousand men plus women and children. From the loaves and fishes of one little boy's lunch He fed them all. On that occasion alone, twenty thousand witnessed the miracle power of Jesus Christ (*see* John 6:1–14).

He stilled a storm (Mark 4:39). He looked at the waves pounding around Him and said, in effect, "It's time for you to cease." And they did. He walked on water (*see* Matthew 14:25). When it came time to pay His taxes, He directed Peter to a fish with the money inside its mouth (*see* Matthew 17:27). Disappointed at finding no fruit on a fig tree, He ordered it to wither up and dry away (*see* Matthew 21:18–22). So it happened. In these and other ways He ordered nature, and nature obeyed.

The Great Physician.   Jesus also showed His miraculous power by healing disease, a second category of miracles. He healed a leper in Luke 5. He healed a paralytic in Mark 2. He healed Peter's mother-in-law in Mark 1. He healed the nobleman's son in John 4. He healed physical illness in John 5. He healed a withered hand in Mark 3. He healed the deaf and dumb in Mark 7. He healed blindness in John 9. He healed ten lepers in Luke 17. And a short time before He was

nailed to the cross, He healed the severed ear of Malchus that
Peter had cut off (*see* Luke 22:49–51).

Back From Death.   A third category of miracles of our Lord
concern His power over the grave. He confronted death and
death yielded up its prey. There was the daughter of Jairus in
Mark 5 and the son of the widow in Luke 7. But the one I love
best is the story of Lazarus in John 11. You remember the
account of how He came to the grave and ordered the stone to
be rolled away. Martha protested. She thought Jesus merely
wanted to pay His respects and to say good-bye. She didn't
understand what was about to happen.
     Prayer. Silence. Then a shout: "Lazarus, come out!" And
Lazarus came out. The people were so shocked that Jesus had
to tell them what to do—unwrap the grave clothes. I don't
know who removed the cloth from Lazarus's face, but I don't
think I could have done it. I would have been immobilized by
shock.

Reactions Ancient and Modern.   Julian the Apostate, a
Roman emperor from 361 to 363, had a vehemently anti-
Christian reaction to Jesus. Philip Schaff, author of *The Person
of Christ,* quotes him as having said, "Jesus . . . has now been
celebrated about 300 years, having done nothing in His
lifetime worthy of fame, unless anyone thinks it a very great
work to heal lame people and blind people and exorcise de-
moniacs in the villages of Bethsaida and Bethany."
     This leads us into another area of the miraculous in Jesus'
life—His power of influence. Consider that the destiny of
every person in the entire world depends upon the Lord Jesus
Christ. There is no salvation outside of Him (*see* Acts 4:12).
Paul declared that "at the name of Jesus every knee should
bow, of things in heaven, and things in earth, and things under
the earth; And that every tongue should confess that Jesus
Christ is Lord, to the glory of God the Father" (Philippians
2:10, 11).

Ernest Renan, the French atheist, said, "Jesus is in every respect unique, and nothing can be compared with him." Napoleon said, "I know men, and I tell you Jesus Christ is no mere man. Between Him and every other man in the world there is no possible term of comparison."

Jesus hit men with an impact unequaled in the history of humanity. After nearly two thousand years the impact is not diminished in any way, but daily there are people who have tremendous revolutionary experiences which they associate with Jesus Christ. The personality of Jesus is without parallel or equal. Is it not astounding that this very day somebody turned his life over to this historical Person who lived two thousand years ago and knew an instant and eternal transformation?

I find that exciting. Some people may think of Jesus as ancient history, but to me He is as alive as anyone I know—even more so. He is the living Christ. He is the master of hungry crowds and angry Pharisees, clever theologians and bitter sinners, stupid disciples and smart governors—Jesus is master of them all.

He is master of Himself. He struggles in the olive groves in the midnight hours before His death. He fights sweat, blood, and tears, and comes forth victorious in complete dedication to God.

In the terrible agony of the cross, He is master. All the people around Him are in fury but He is calm and in control. Listen to His words as He dies. He passes forgiveness on to a penitent thief and opens the doors of Paradise to him. He remembers His dear mother and His beloved friend John. When the effects of the loss of blood, shock, trauma, exposure, and the torture of crucifixion finally get to Him, He calmly fulfills the last prophecy by saying, "I thirst" (John 19:28). In obedience to the Father's will, He yields Himself to death. (The details of His death are discussed and documented in my book *Can a Man Live Again?*, Moody Press, 1975.)

No one has ever been born the way Christ was born. No one

has ever lived as He lived. No one has ever died as He died. There is no one to compare with Him. He has influenced the world.

Signed, Sealed, and Delivered. Jesus said and promised amazing things:

> I am the way, the truth, and the life: no man cometh unto the Father, but by me . . . The Son of man hath power upon earth to forgive sins . . . Whosoever therefore shall confess me before men, him will I confess also before my Father which is in heaven . . . No man knoweth the Son, but the Father; neither knoweth any man the Father, save the Son, and he to whomsoever the Son shall reveal him . . . I am the resurrection, and the life: he that believeth in me, though he were dead, yet shall he live: And whosoever liveth and believeth in me shall never die . . . Whosoever will lose his life for my sake shall find it . . . I am the light of the world: he that followeth me shall not walk in darkness, but shall have the light of life . . . Whosoever drinketh of the water that I shall give him shall never thirst . . . Come unto me, all ye that labour and are heavy laden, and I will give you rest . . . Heaven and earth shall pass away, but my words shall not pass away . . . Before Abraham was, I am . . . Upon this rock I will build my church; and the gates of hell shall not prevail against it . . . I am the door of the sheep. All that ever came before me are thieves and robbers . . . I and my Father are one . . . I am the bread of life: he that cometh to me shall never hunger.

What a striking collection of verses—promises from the miraculous Jesus!

Victory Over Death. We referred to Jesus raising the dead. But we also see His miraculous working in His own Resurrection. Do you know He ordered His own death? Hanging there on the cross, according to John 19:28, He just watched the prophecy being fulfilled. As part of the fulfillment He said, "I thirst," and then He died. From the grave He controlled His own burial, making sure that those attending to this placed His body at the right time in the right place—this, too, to fulfill prophecy. (This is also documented in my book *Can a Man Live Again?*)

And when the time came for Him to leave the grave, He left. The tomb is empty. It has been empty since those initial three days. There is abundant Scripture and historical evidence to support the Resurrection of Christ. Should that be surprising? Death is a natural consequence, but God is supernatural. And Christ not only conquered death for Himself but for us as well. Because He lives, we shall live also.

To Be Expected. As we look at the life and miracles of Jesus, we can only conclude that He was God. And if we accept that proposition, all else logically follows. If God became man, we would expect Him to have a unique and miraculous entrance into this world. Jesus did.

If God became man, we would expect Him to be sinless and to live a godly life. Jesus did.

If God became man, we would anticipate His words to be the clearest, the most authoritative, the truest and purest words ever spoken. Jesus' words were.

If God became man, we would expect Him to manifest supernatural power. Jesus did that.

If God became man, we would expect Him to have a universal and permanent influence on the lives of men. Jesus does.

If God became man, we would expect Him to exercise power over death. Jesus did.

God *did* become man. His name was Jesus of Nazareth—Jesus the Christ, worker of miracles!

8

Science and the Bible

Many have taken upon themselves the task of making statements about the Bible and science. Aldous Huxley said, "Modern science makes it impossible to believe in a personal God." Philosopher Bertrand Russell said:

> Man is the product of causes which had no pre-vision of the end they were achieving. His origin, his growth, his hopes, his fears, his loves and beliefs are but the outcome of accidental collocation of atoms; . . . that all the labors of the ages are destined to extinction in the vast death of the solar system . . . if not quite beyond dispute, are yet so certain that no philosophy which rejects them can hope to stand.

It seems that as science advances and verifies more and more data and more and more technology, there is a movement on the part of some scientists to eliminate the necessity of God. Once God was almighty; now science is almighty. Some scientists who hold to a position called *scientism* continue to assent that as they find explanations of natural phenomena, God becomes smaller and smaller.

Must It Be Either-Or? Christians are constantly being confronted with a supposed conflict between science and Scripture. We are told that Christianity is scientifically unrespected and that it doesn't gain the respect of a scientific world because it makes nonscientific statements and blunders. The worldlings say that you have to choose science or religion, that you can't have both. Either the "facts of science" or the "fantasy of Scripture"—you must decide.

And so the clash goes on, based on the fact that both science and the Scripture claim total authority. But let me suggest that there is no real conflict between science and Scripture—none. A great difference exists between science and scientism. Scientism constitutes the theories of a scientist who is wearing glasses with philosophically tinted lenses.

No, there is no real conflict between the Bible and science. You can be a Christian and at the same time be a very capable scientist. For example, many outstanding men were respected both as Christians and as scientists: Galileo, Kepler, Descartes, von Leibnitz, Newton, and Pascal, to name only a few.

What's in a Word?   It is true that the Bible doesn't use scientific jargon, but that doesn't make the Bible nonscientific. Suppose you are enjoying a Thanksgiving Day turkey, and someone asks, "Would you like more?" In scientific language you might reply, "Gastronomical satiety admonishes me that I have arrived at a state of deglutition consistent with dietetic integrity." Which means, "No, thanks, I've had enough!"

You do not expect the Bible to make statements such as that. Instead, the Bible talks in everyday language. We do not disparage the Word of God and say it is nonscientific because it doesn't use current scientific terminology.

Once we get over that hurdle of terminology, it can be pointed out that there is no real conflict between science and Scripture. The conflict comes when science stops being science and starts being religion. Science, by its very definition, can only deal with that which is observable, that which is reproducible. Whenever it gets beyond reproducible, experimental fact and starts trying to talk about origins and destinies, it becomes religion. It is jumping to things that cannot be observed. That is where the conflict lies.

Yet many Christians assume that the Bible is full of scientific error. The whole movement known as neoorthodoxy has already bowed to this concept. Its proponents agree that the Bible is full of scientific error, so they have given up on it. The typical neoorthodox statement runs this way: "The Bible is only authoritative when it speaks on spiritual matters. When it speaks on scientific matters, we have to handle it allegorically and spiritually, because it is prone to error." That is merely a claim that the God who wrote the Bible knew a lot about spiritual things but didn't know anything about science.

A Double Out.   To say that the parts of the Bible that talk about spiritual things are true and the parts that talk about science are false is ridiculous for two reasons.

Number one, it denies the inspiration of God in the Scripture. If God is God, then He knows as much about science as He does about spiritual things.

Number two, it denies the inerrancy of Scripture, that the Bible has been properly recorded. If God wrote this Book and if God wrote it correctly, it is inspired and inerrant. In that case it is just as right scientifically as it is spiritually. God can only speak truth: ". . . thy Word is truth" (John 17:17). The New Testament declares that God cannot lie (*see* Titus 1:2). And there is nothing that He does not know. He is omniscient. When science sets itself against God's revelation, it ceases to be science. It becomes ignorance. It becomes an ignorant religion.

The scientist who practices scientism isn't content to observe what is going on *now*. He has got to extrapolate everything into the past and everything into the future and discuss origins and destinies. But he can't do that because it isn't science. He can't put the past into a test tube because the past isn't reproducible. Science can only observe the present—that is all. It can only deal with the observable activity of a microscope or telescope or test tube.

While it is true that the scientist has some past history of tests and experiments to lean on, he inevitably wants to go back into prehistory. But when he starts going back behind his recorded history, he is talking about what is nonobservable. It

is not reproducible. It cannot be made scientific. So his speculations about prehistoric origins become, for him, a matter of
faith.

Always the Same?   As an example of how science works, consider the theory called uniformity, which says that everything
going on at the present rate has always gone on at the same
rate and will always continue to go on at the same rate.

So the scientist goes through his experiment of natural processes today, and he says it takes such and such a time to do
this and to do that. Then he goes backward and extrapolates
his uniformity concept. Holding to the idea that everything in
the past proceeded at the same rate it does in the present, he
concludes that man is millions of years old and that the earth
is billions of years old.

But does he really know that? No, because he has no information about the prehistoric past. Very little was written before the Old Testament period. And back then, people were
people. They were not hanging in trees by their tails and they
were not in the process of becoming human.

It is impossible for us to prove scientifically that the scientist is wrong at this point. A Christian can't say, "You've struck
out, fellows. I'm going to show you your error." That can't be
done because the events of the past are not reproducible.
They are not subject to scientific checking. Evolution can't be
reproduced, but neither can creation.

Another View?   "Well," you may ask, "what does the Bible
teach about this matter?" God acted in great catastrophies.

Catastrophism. (There are several books that deal with the
subject of catastrophism. Among the very helpful ones are *The
Genesis Flood* by John Whitcomb and Henry Morris and
Many Infallible Proofs by Henry Morris.) The Bible teaches
that in six days God made everything. The Bible denies the
theory of uniformity as a valid explanation of what has happened or what is going to happen. The Word of God declares
that in the past the heavens and the earth were created. And

the same Word declares that in the future Jesus is going to return and create a new heaven and a new earth.

The Scripture's view on this comes through Peter. He wrote:

> There shall come in the last days scoffers, walking after their own lusts, And saying, Where is the promise of his coming? for since the fathers fell asleep, all things continue as they were from the beginning of the creation. For this they willingly are ignorant of, that by the word of God the heavens were of old, and the earth standing out of the water and in the water: Whereby the world that then was, being overflowed with water, perished: But the heavens and the earth, which are now, by the same word are kept in store, reserved unto fire against the day of judgment and perdition of ungodly men.
>
> 2 Peter 3:3–7

Peter is pointing out that those people who think that all things are going to continue as they were in the past have forgotten that that is not true. Have they forgotten the Flood in the days of Noah? Are they forgetting the fiery day of judgment to come? The Bible is saying that the theory of uniformity just doesn't hold water, if I may be allowed a pun. Instead, the theory of catastrophism is laid out for us. It explains the rock strata. It explains all the scientific facts and data, and fits in beautifully with what God has set forth in His Word.

Everything boils down to this: Either we believe in the uniformity that can't be proven, or we believe in catastrophism, which the Bible defends.

With that in mind, I repeat that there is no conflict between science and the Bible. There is only conflict on a moral basis between men and God. Ungodly men don't like to retain God in their knowledge, as the Bible says in Romans 1:28. So they hold to their doctrine of uniformity and that, I say, takes greater faith than to believe in the Bible.

A good illustration is found in a newsletter in which one scientist candidly admits, "I reject the idea of a transcendent God, so what other option do I have? That's what I believe in." That shows that his decision is a moral one, not one based on science.

The issue is not between science and Scripture. The issue is whether or not a man wants to submit to the Word of God. Most have rejected God, and so they have to come up with some explanation. They reject revelation for imagination. If God didn't create, they reason, then all this "just happened."

How Science Works. Scientists generally agree and hold to several basic principles. First, science must deal with *things*—that is, matter. Second, science must deal with *happenings*—that is, energy. Third, science must deal with a matrix in which those things happen—that is, *space-time*. So the basics of science are matter, energy, and space-time. The universe in essence, then, must be a continuum of matter, energy, space, and time. Science tells us that one of these cannot exist without the other. All three must work together. This continuum must have existed simultaneously from the beginning of life.

As we saw that is exactly what you have in Genesis 1:1. "In the beginning God created the heaven and the earth." That includes matter, energy, and the space-time matrix. The first verse of the Bible has God creating the three basic dimensions of science simultaneously!

Once the universe had been created in its processes, scientists say, they were designed to operate in an orderly fashion. All the different phenomena were ordered and sustained by these forces. Science says that the forces continue and continue and continue. No further creation was needed.

That is what the Bible says, too: ". . . God ended his work which he had made . . ." (Genesis 2:2). God in the beginning put everything right simultaneously, and when He put it all together, He stopped and the Creation ended right there. Matter is never totally lost. Energy is never totally lost. Time and space continue.

The complete cessation of creative activity has been recognized by modern science as the first law of thermodynamics. It is the law of the conservation of mass and energy, one of the most universal and most certain of all scientific principles. Science has shown that there is nothing being created in the known universe at this time. Changes are occurring that affect matter and energy, but nothing is being created now. And the Bible says that when God ended His work, He ended it! That fits the scientific facts.

Written in the Word. The Bible, of course, supports the first law of thermodynamics. For example, read Isaiah 40:26: "Lift up your eyes on high, and behold who hath created these things, that bringeth out their host by number: he calleth them all by names by the greatness of his might, for that he is strong in power; not one faileth." Here is the law of the conservation of mass and energy.

Scientists "discovered" what they called the first law of thermodynamics. They really just discovered the truth of Isaiah 40:26.

Read Nehemiah 9:6: "Thou, even thou, art Lord alone; thou hast made heaven, the heaven of heavens, with all their host, the earth, and all things that are therein, the seas, and all that is therein, *and thou preservest them all . . .*" (author's italics).

Even Solomon recognized this as seen in Ecclesiastes 1:9: "The thing that hath been, it is that which shall be; and that which is done is that which shall be done: and there is no new thing under the sun." And here is yet another clear statement about the continuation of creation: "Is there any thing whereof it may be said, See, this is new? it hath been already of old time, which was before us" (verse 10).

Science says the totality of mass and energy occurred because of evolution. Believers say that God made it, but notice that at least they both agree on the truth of the conservation of matter and energy. Ecclesiastes 3:14, 15 says, "I know that, whatsoever God doeth, it shall be for ever: nothing can be put to it, nor any thing taken from it . . . . That which hath been is now; and that which is to be hath already been . . . ." Isn't that amazing? The Word of God is absolutely accurate in defending and defining the first law of thermodynamics, the conservation of mass and energy.

Law Number Two. There is a second law of thermodynamics, the law of increasing disorder. It says that although there is never a loss of mass and energy, its ability to produce and to make a productive contribution breaks down and down and down. Order becomes disorder. All processes will finally cease and the universe will be dead, scientists tell us.

"Does that fit Scripture?" you ask.

It certainly does. But God didn't make the world with the second law of thermodynamics operating. God made the world and He looked at it and said, "It is good." But when man sinned, the second law of thermodynamics came into being.

Science has never been able to figure out how that law works or where it came from. But we know it came from the Fall of Man. After man fell, God said, ". . . cursed is the ground . . ." (Genesis 3:17). That was simply the symbol of the curse that stretched everywhere.

If you want a good explanation of where the second law of thermodynamics came from, check Romans 8:

> For the creature [creation] was made subject to vanity, not willingly, but by reason of him who hath subjected the same in hope, Because the creature itself also shall be delivered from the bondage of corruption into the glorious liberty of the children of God. For we know that the whole creation groaneth and travaileth in pain together until now.
>
> Verses 20–22, author's brackets

At present we have disorder, a breaking down, an entropy existing in nature. But Romans 8:20–22 tells us that this condition is only temporary. Why? Because the Lord is going to come and create a new heaven and a new earth. There will be no second law of thermodynamics operating in the kingdom of God.

I like that! The Bible promises no more curse, no more death, no more tears, no more sorrow, no more crying, no more pain, no more regrets, no more exile, no more trouble, no more hurting, no more destruction, no more decay, no more unrighteousness, no more night, no more sin! That is a big collection of "no mores."

For me, the second law of thermodynamics is completely explained by the curse that came upon man and his world.

The Water Cycle. Hydrology is basically the science that deals with the cycles followed by the waters of the earth. Simply stated, water from the ocean is evaporated up into the atmosphere and collected in the clouds. Then it is redeposited on the earth as rain or snow. Water from this rain and snow runs into streams, then rivers, and eventually winds up in the ocean. Water evaporates from the ocean, and the cycle just keeps going on and on. Part of the rain and snow that falls seeps into the ground, and therefore we have the water table that is in the ground, which provides water as well.

This whole cycle of hydrology puzzled the world until the seventeenth century. Until then, in fact, people believed in subterranean reservoirs, which were supposed to exist deep in the middle of the earth. That is where the springs were thought to come from.

But study in this area in the seventeenth century opened up the modern concept of hydrology. Science had at last discovered and defined the evaporation and transportation and precipitation aspects of the water cycle.

Centuries earlier, if people had only read Isaiah 55, they would have had the problem solved for them; "For as the rain and the snow come down from heaven, And do not return there . . . ." But don't stop reading now because nothing is said about a cycle. Read on: ". . . without watering the earth, And making it bear and sprout, And furnishing seed to the sower and bread to the eater" (verse 10 NAS). Now there is the cycle. God deposits the rain, it saturates the earth, is recollected, evaporated, brought up from the seas and from the dry land and cycled back to the clouds again. That is scientifically accurate. And incidentally, the Word of God has this same cycle effect, for God used the hydrology information to illustrate the effectiveness of His Word: "So shall my word be that goeth forth out of my mouth: it shall not return unto me void, but it shall accomplish that which I please, and it shall prosper in the thing whereto I sent it" (verse 11).

Ecclesiastes 1:6, 7 provide more information: "The wind goeth toward the south, and turneth about unto the north; it whirleth about continually, and the wind returneth again according to his circuits. All the rivers run into the sea; yet the sea is not full; unto the place from whence the rivers come, thither they return again." Do you know why the sea doesn't become full, even though all the rivers keep running into it? Because it is the same water. It just keeps going around and around and around. Solomon pointed that out a long time before the seventeenth century, but nobody picked it up.

Read also Job 36: "For he maketh small the drops of water: they pour down rain according to the vapour thereof: Which the clouds do drop and distil upon man abundantly" (verses 27, 28). The oldest book in the Bible describes the process of evaporation and precipitation.

Psalms 135:7 tells us that God "causeth the vapours to ascend from the ends of the earth; he maketh lightnings for the rain; he bringeth the wind out of his treasuries." So the Scripture gives the hydrological cycle and the features of evaporation.

You can read Job 26:8 and find out about condensation. You can read Job 28:10 and find out about the runoff of water. Psalms 33:7 tells about the ocean reservoirs. And Job 38:22

asks, "Hast thou entered into the treasures of the snow? or hast thou seen the treasures of the hail?" Clouds store snow and hail? So the Bible long ago set forth facts that men have begun to understand only recently. But God made the whole hydrological cycle, and told us about it in His Word.

Look Up. For another illustration of why Bible and science do not conflict, let us go to astronomy. Modern astronomy, which is the study of the solar system, didn't begin to replace the old ideas until the seventeenth century. The prevalent theory before then stated that the earth was round and flat. People said that if you were dumb enough to sail through the Pillars of Hercules, which is the Rock of Gibraltar, you would fall off into nothingness.

When Copernicus (1473–1543) came along and presented his theory that the earth was in motion, people thought he was out of his mind. Then came men such as Brahe, Kepler, and Galileo (1564–1642) in the seventeenth century. They gave birth to modern astronomy, which tells us of the infinite size and variety of the universe. They conceived of the universe as staggering in size and endless.

Were they the first to learn that? The Prophet Isaiah talked about how high the heavens were above the earth, in quoting the Lord (*see* Isaiah 55:9). The oldest book in the Bible asked and exclaimed, "Is not God in the height of heaven? and behold the height of the stars, how high they are!" (Job 22:12).

Jeremiah referred to the solar system as vast and distant: "Thus saith the Lord; If heaven above can be measured, and the foundations of the earth searched out beneath, I will also cast off all the seed of Israel for all that they have done, saith the Lord" (Jeremiah 31:37).

Before the telescope was invented in the seventeenth century, Hippartus said there were 1,022 stars. But Ptolemy said, "You missed it. The number is 1,056." Then Kepler said, "You're both wrong, fellows. There are exactly 1,055." Jeremiah testifies, "The host of heaven cannot be counted

. . ." (Jeremiah 33:22 NAS). Today scientists tell us there are
more than 100 billion stars in our galaxy alone. And how many
billion galaxies there are, nobody knows! There is no more
way of counting the stars than there is of counting the grains of
sand on the shores of this earth.

Science has also recently discovered that stars are all different. The Bible has been saying that all along: "There is one
glory of the sun, and another glory of the moon, and another
glory of the stars: for one star differeth from another star in
glory" (1 Corinthians 15:41). Now if the Bible had said, "All
the stars are the same," then you could set the Bible aside as
wrong. But the Word of God is not wrong—in this or in any
other point. It never makes a mistake. God knows as much
about stars as He does about salvation.

Written in the Rocks.   Let me suggest another area—geology,
the science of the earth. Consider the field called isostasy—
the study of the balance of the earth. This wasn't fully understood until about 1959. The earth has been found to be perfectly balanced with an equal weight to support land mass,
mountains, valleys, and water. The equilibrium of all this is
nothing less than astounding.

For example, the ocean exerts a pressure against the shore
that keeps the mountains up. Rock masses have different
weights at different places to balance it out. That is a fairly
recent discovery. But do you know what Isaiah wrote long
ago? "Who [God] hath measured the waters in the hollow of
his hand, and meted out heaven with the span, and com-
prehended the dust of the earth in a measure, and weighed
the mountains in scales, and the hills in a balance?" (Isaiah
40:12, author's brackets). Who else but God?

"He [God] established the earth upon its foundations, So
that it will not totter forever and ever" (Psalms 104:5 NAS,
author's brackets). "The mountains rose; the valleys sank
down to the place which Thou didst establish for them" (verse
8). God made the earth so that it balanced.

Again and again I find that there is no contradiction between science and the Bible. The same God who wrote the Bible is the God who made the world and the universe.

Day and Night. The concept of a round earth helps us to interpret an interesting passage in the New Testament. Referring to the Second Coming, or just prior to it, Luke wrote:

> In that day, he which shall be upon the housetop, and his stuff in the house, let him not come down to take it away: and he that is in the field, let him likewise not return back. Remember Lot's wife. Whosoever shall seek to save his life shall lose it; and whosoever shall lose his life shall preserve it. I tell you, in that night there shall be two men in one bed; the one shall be taken, and the other shall be left.
>
> Luke 17:31–34

If you look at those verses carefully, you will notice that the word *day* is used and then two verses later the word *night* is used. How can it be day and night at the same time when the Lord returns? Only one way—because of the existence of a spherical globe. That would explain how some could be working and some sleeping. Anybody who thought that the earth was flat didn't understand the significance of Luke 17.

In the seventeenth century John Newton defined the law of gravity. But thousands of years before, Job had said, "He . . . hangeth the earth upon nothing" (Job 26:7).

Talk About the Weather. The Bible is accurate not only in areas such as hydrology, astronomy, and geology but also in meteorology, the basic principle of which is the circulation of the atmosphere. In the seventeenth century Galileo discovered that wind travels in circuitous patterns. Galileo was a little behind Solomon, who lived about 900 B.C. Solomon said,

"The wind goeth toward the south, and turneth about unto the north; it whirleth about continually, and the wind returneth again according to his circuits" (Ecclesiastes 1:6).

Before Galileo no scientist had determined that air had weight. But the Book of Job said long before that, "He [God] imparted weight to the wind . . ." (Job 28:25 NAS, author's brackets). Again, the Bible is accurate when it speaks on science.

A Look at the Body. The Bible is accurate in the science of physiology. William Harvey in 1628 discovered that the circulatory system is the key to life. Only then was it understood that circulation of the blood is what keeps a person alive. Before that, whenever someone got sick, the doctor took blood out through a bleeding process. But now doctors give blood to the sick because they know that blood makes for life. That agrees with Leviticus 17:11 which says, "The life of the flesh is in the blood."

"That verse is referring to a spiritual truth," you may say. Yes, it does refer to the ancient sacrificial system, but it is scientifically correct as relating to physical life as well. The Bible doesn't make mistakes. Essentially in all of the illustrations I have given it is spiritual truth that is the issue. But when the Scripture, making its spiritual point, touches on a scientific theme, it is just as inerrant at that juncture as in the spiritual.

In 1953 a medical book came out entitled *Personality Manifestations and Psychosomatic Illness.* It discussed how emotions can cause debilitating and even fatal illnesses. The book diagramed the emotional center of the brain from which nerve fibers descend to every area of the body. The diagram demonstrated how emotional trauma, any emotional stress or turmoil in the emotional center, can send out impulses through the fibers of the nerve system and can cause anything from headaches to foot itch and far more serious things.

The book said the emotional center produces illness in

three ways. First, it changes the amount of blood flow. For example, when a person gets mad, the blood rushes to his face. Emotional stress can increase the amount or decrease the amount of blood flow, and consequently can cause disease.

Second, emotional stress at the center of the nervous system can affect secretions of certain glands. Have you ever been very nervous before you were to give a speech—so much so that your mouth dried up? Your brain sent certain impulses through your nervous system that dried up the glands that provide fluid in your mouth.

What happens when you get excess pressure through emotional stress? For example, excess thyroxin is produced by emotion. When too much thyroxin is poured into the bloodstream it can produce goiter and even fatal heart disease.

Third, emotions can change physical health by creating muscle tension. The nerves affect the muscles and the muscles tighten up and become tense.

The Word of God anticipated what science has so recently discovered about the relationship of emotions to physical health. Check Proverbs 16:24: "Pleasant words are as an honeycomb, sweet to the soul, and health to the bones." You see, God knew that emotional stress—anger, criticism, and sour words—can affect physical health. God revealed it: "A merry heart doeth good like a medicine: but a broken spirit drieth the bones" (Proverbs 17:22). A happy person is a healthy person. An unhappy person is an unhealthy person.

Thy Word Is Truth. We have lightly touched on the areas of hydrology, astronomy, geology, meteorology, and physiology. And if space permitted we could delve into biology, archaeology, anthropology, and all the other "ologies." We would find that each time the Bible speaks on these areas, it is absolutely accurate in what it has to say. Things that scientists have only recently discovered were declared in the Bible long ago.

How can this be? There is only one answer. God is the author of this Book and the revealer of the truth it contains.

Instead of refuting Scripture, science, properly understood, confirms it. To pit science against the Bible is foolish and unnecessary. I am convinced that in the final analysis all truth—scientific and spiritual—is one. As Jesus said, ". . . thy word is truth" (John 17:17). The Bible speaks the truth at all points because God inspired its writing.

9

Writing History Before
It Happens

One of the great marks of divine revelation is prophecy
(used here in the sense of prediction). God has written down
in this Book events in history—people, places, and the
conflicts of both—with such absolute accuracy that there is no
way that the human mind could ever have foretold them. Only
the divine mind of God could have foreseen them.

This is essentially the argument from omniscience. Only
God who knows all could give us, detail by detail, history
before it happened. And this is precisely what the Bible does.

Prophecy is a declaration of future events which no human
wisdom or prediction is capable of making because it depends
on a knowledge of the innumerable contingencies of human
affairs which belong exclusively to the omniscience of God.
So from its very nature prophecy must be divine revelation.
Prophecy is not merely a good guess. Prophecy is not just
conjecture. It is the statement of historical fact that is unpre-
dictable and unknowable except to God.

Now some people insist that fulfilled prophecy doesn't
prove the Bible is the Word of God. Well, unfulfilled or wrong
prophecy could surely prove in a hurry that the Bible *isn't* the
Word of God. The divine standard for prophecy is given to us
in Deuteronomy 18: "But the prophet, which shall presume to
speak a word in my name, which I have not commanded him
to speak, or that shall speak in the name of other gods, even
that prophet shall die" (verse 20). God doesn't tolerate false
prophets. "And if thou say in thine heart, How shall we

know the word which the Lord hath not spoken? When a prophet speaketh in the name of the Lord, if the thing follow not, nor come to pass, that is the thing which the Lord hath not spoken, but the prophet hath spoken it presumptuously: thou shalt not be afraid of him" (verses 21, 22).

The standard for God's prophets was absolute accuracy. If therefore we find one prophecy in the Bible that didn't come to pass as the Bible said, then we can set aside the Bible as being unreliable.

From the Beginning. Do you know that the first Christian sermon ever preached was based on prophecy? We read in the Book of Acts that Peter stood up before the crowd on the Day of Pentecost and said that God had determined that Christ would die. Immediately he launched into the prophecies of the Book of Psalms as they related to the Messiah. The preaching of the other apostles and of the Early Church leaders centered frequently on prophetic themes. Fulfilled prophecy has always been a part of Christian preaching.

Prophecy in the Bible covers a very broad area. Some relates to large groups of people; some to individuals; some to rulers; some to cities; some to nations; some to the whole world.

Great portions of the Bible are devoted to prophecy. In the Old Testament, for example, there are twenty consecutive chapters of prophecy in Isaiah, seventeen in Jeremiah, nine in Ezekiel, and two in Amos. They predict doom for Amon, Moab, Edom, Philistia, Babylon, Tyre, Sidon, and so on.

Named Before Birth. Isaiah sat down one day to write, under the inspiration of the Holy Spirit, about a man who at that time had not been born: "That saith of Cyrus, He is my shepherd, and shall perform all my pleasure: even saying to Jerusalem, Thou shalt be built; and to the temple, Thy foundation shall be laid" (Isaiah 44:28). In modern terms, the prophet might have said, "Folks, a man is coming who is going to release the

Jews from captivity and send them back to Jerusalem to build the wall and to build the Temple. His name is Cyrus." How could Isaiah say that about Cyrus 150 years before he was born?

"It was a good guess!" you say. Are we to believe that the mother of Cyrus in later years read the prophecy and had a child whom she named Cyrus and whose life she then planned to fulfill that prophecy? Not likely. She was a pagan. Surely she had no knowledge of such a prophecy. Neither she nor anyone else could possibly guess that Cyrus was going to be king and release Israel.

Another example of name-before-birth concerned Josiah. We read in 1 Kings 13:2, ". . . Behold, a child shall be born unto the house of David, Josiah by name; and upon thee shall he offer the priests of the high places that burn incense upon thee, and men's bones shall be burnt upon thee." Now that prophecy was given three hundred years before Josiah was born. He was named in advance and it was foretold what he would do. And that was exactly how it turned out. No man could have known this in advance. It had to be revealed by God.

God invited people to test the accuracy of His Word. It can stand scrutiny. It has never been wrong. And since it proves to be right, we had better listen to it. Our Lord said, "Take ye heed: behold, I have foretold you all things" (Mark 13:23). He said that in a prophetic context to show us who He was and to call our attention to what He had to say.

Tyre Retired.   The Bible contains many examples of fulfilled prophecy. One concerns the city of Tyre on the Mediterranean Sea. The story is in Ezekiel 26:

> Therefore thus saith the Lord God; Behold, I am against thee, O Tyrus, and will cause many nations to come up against thee, as the sea causeth his waves to come up. And they shall destroy the walls of Tyrus, and

break down her towers: I will also scrape her dust from
her, and make her like the top of a rock. It shall be a
place for the spreading of nets in the midst of the sea:
for I have spoken it, saith the Lord God: and it shall
become a spoil to the nations.

Verses 3–5

Who is going to do this? A man named Nebuchadnezzar,
king of Babylon (*see* verse 7). How he is going to do it?

He shall slay with the sword thy daughters in the
field: and he shall make a fort against thee, and cast a
mount against thee, and lift up the buckler against thee.
And he shall set engines of war against thy walls, and
with his axes he shall break down thy towers.

Verses 8, 9

What will be the end result of this military action?

And I will make thee like the top of a rock: thou shalt
be a place to spread nets upon; thou shalt be built no
more: for I the Lord have spoken it, saith the Lord God
. . . . I will make thee a terror, and thou shalt be no
more: though thou be sought for, yet shalt thou never be
found again, saith the Lord God.

Verses 14, 21

Could It Happen?   Now Tyre wasn't just a little fishing vil-
lage. It was one of the great cities of Phoenicia. You recall
from history that the Phoenicians were the great colonizers
and mariners of ancient times. They navigated around Africa
and established trade routes to the East.

They built themselves a magnificent city with strongly fortified walls 150 feet high and 15 feet thick. The walls protected the land side of the city and navy vessels protected the
city from the sea.

Both David and Solomon looked to Tyre for materials and artisans in their great building projects. The great cedars of Lebanon came through that area. So Tyre was important in biblical history as well as secular history.

Year After Year. Three years after Ezekiel had given this prophecy against Tyre, Nebuchadnezzar came down from the north and did exactly what was predicted. He began a siege of the city and threw up a mound against the city walls. Military tactics back in those days called for cutting off the traffic, trade, supplies, and food to a city, and starving the defenders out. Nebuchadnezzar's siege lasted thirteen years. At the end of that time he stormed the city and smashed the walls. He broke down the towers as Ezekiel had predicted. Smashing the towers of a city wasn't always done at the conclusion of a siege, but it was in this case.

When Nebuchadnezzar finally fought his way into the city, he found no spoils because the citizens of Tyre had removed everything of value to a little island one-half mile offshore. And there they sat in safety, thumbing their noses at the king of Babylon. Nebuchadnezzar went back home, and the new little community sitting out in the sea flourished for the next 250 years.

Only part of Ezekiel's prophecy had been fulfilled. True, the city had been destroyed and the walls and towers broken down. But what about the stones and timber and dust being thrown into the water? That had not happened.

Finishing It Off. But then a young man named Alexander the Great came upon the scene. He had defeated the Persians, the second of the world empires foretold by the Prophet Daniel. And now he was out to conquer the world. He arrived in Phoenician territory with thirty-three thousand infantry, fifteen thousand cavalry, and a few ships sailing along the coast. He asked the city of Tyre to open its gates to him, but the people refused. They felt secure on their tiny island, which by now had been fortified with a high wall.

Alexander knew that the only way to approach Tyre would be on a land peninsula stretching out to the island. So he set about building a causeway some two hundred feet wide stretching out for a half mile.

It was a very difficult task, as you can well imagine. For material he used what was left of the original city of Tyre. He took the stones and the bricks of the tower and began to toss them into the sea. As the water got deeper and deeper, the project seemed more and more impossible.

To make matters worse, the Tyrians sat on their high walls and began bombarding the Greeks with missiles. To protect his operation, Alexander built mobile protecting shields. The soldiers and workmen kept these overhead as they moved closer and closer to the walls.

Alexander recognized that once he reached the island city he would still have the walls to contend with. So he constructed what have been called helepoleis. They were a group of 160-foot-high towers that could be moved on wheels. The idea was to roll these big, lumbering monsters right out on the causeway and up against the walls, then flop down a drawbridge and march right across the top of the wall into the city.

The fact that Alexander was using the rubble of the original city to build his causeway was fulfilling prophecy, which said that the site would be scraped bare. But what about the prophecy saying that many nations would come against Tyre?

Well, as Alexander was building the land bridge, he was being attacked by ships of Tyre on both sides. Alexander saw that he needed ships so that he could defend his flanks. So he went back to the cities and nations he had previously conquered and demanded that they provide him with vessels. He gathered a fleet from Sidon, Byblos, Rhodes, Macedon, and other places. So just as Ezekiel had said, many nations were coming against Tyre.

Down and Out.   At last the causeway to Tyre was complete. Alexander rolled out his big towers and pushed them against the wall. The drawbridges were lowered and the Greek soldiers swarmed into the city. In the battle eight thousand

people of Tyre were slain. Another seven thousand were exe-
cuted and thirty thousand were sold into slavery. The city
itself was completely destroyed. This impossible victory had
been won in just seven months. The prophecy of Ezekiel had
been carried out.

What about the statement, however, that the city would
never again be rebuilt? Philip Myers, a historian, says, "Alexander the Great reduced Tyre to ruins in 332 B.C. She recov-
ered in a measure but never to the place she previously held
in the world." Myers goes on to say that the once great city is
now as bare as the top of a rock. It is a place where fishermen
dry their nets.

Jerusalem has been rebuilt seventeen times, but Tyre has
never been rebuilt. Why? Because twenty-five centuries ago a
Jew in Babylon prophesied, "Thou shalt never be rebuilt."
Today the ancient site of Tyre would be an excellent location
for a city. It is a beautiful place, well situated, and has a tremendous fresh-water supply capable of supplying a city. But it
hasn't been rebuilt, and it won't be.

Do you know what the probability of all the prophecies
against Tyre coming true would be? Peter Stoner, a
mathematician, figured it as 1 chance in 75 million. Yet, "They
all came true in the minutest detail," he said in his book *Science Speaks.*

All About Nineveh. Nineveh was one of the great cities of
the ancient world and the capital of the Assyrian empire. It
had a 100-foot-high inner wall that was 50 feet thick. Towers
went as high as 200 feet. It had fifteen gates and a 150-foot
moat. The city was walled in for a seven-mile circumference.

Nineveh had a double wall, the outer wall about 2,000 feet
from the inner wall. So to get into the heart of the city one had
to get over the outer wall, go one-half mile, cross a 150-foot
moat, and then scale a 100-foot wall protected by 200-foot
towers. That was quite a fortification. The people of Nineveh,
which reached its high point in history in 663 B.C., felt safe.

But anyone who knew Bible prophecy would not have felt
safe. The whole Book of Nahum centered on Nineveh:

But with an overrunning flood he will make an utter
end of the place thereof, and darkness shall pursue his
enemies. What do ye imagine against the Lord? he will
make an utter end: affliction shall not rise up the second
time. For while they be folden together as thorns, and
while they are drunken as drunkards, they shall be de-
voured as stubble fully dry.

                                              Nahum 1:8–10

So God was going to deal with Nineveh just once. While the
people were having their orgies and drunken brawls the
enemy was going to come in and wipe out the city in one
blow. How would all this happen? With an overrunning flood:
"The gates of the rivers shall be opened, and the palace shall
be dissolved" (Nahum 2:6). You see, rivers ran through cities
in those days. Of course, they had to put an area in the wall
where the river would come through and then they would put
iron gates through the river and the water would flow through
the gates. But in a flood, the gates would wash away. When
there were no gates, there was no protection. History tells us
that this is exactly what came to pass. The gates of Nineveh
were carried away with a great flood, and the Medes and the
Persians entered the city and took it.

God also said, "There is no healing of thy bruise; thy wound
is grievous . . ." (Nahum 3:19). In other words, the city was
not to be rebuilt, and it never has been. There is no Nineveh
today.

True in the Past, True in the Future. Now what does all this
fulfilled prophecy of the past—and we could give many more
examples—mean to us today? It underscores the fact that the
Bible is true. If it is true in what it says about Tyre and
Nineveh, that is strong evidence that it is true in what it tells
us about Jesus Christ, about sin, about heaven and hell. Just as
the prophecies of the past have come to pass, so will those of
the future. Just as God has judged people and cities and nations for rejecting Him in the past, so will He judge men for

rejecting Him in the future. That is a warning for the unsaved to get right with God, and for those who are believers already to get down to business in serving Him, to bow to the Lordship of Jesus Christ.

This Book is true. We can bank our lives on it. Here is our strong confidence. May we love the truth of the Bible, know it, and share it with others.

10

Which Way to God?

The ultimate issue in this whole matter of the Bible comes down to God's wisdom versus man's wisdom (philosophy). We have been looking at many evidences that strongly support the claim that the Bible is the divine revelation of God. Why do unregenerate men reject God's revelation and try to explain away the things this little volume touches on? The reason is their humanistic philosophy. Human wisdom always sets itself against the Gospel. It wants no part of Christ or the cross.

Whenever philosophy gets mixed with revelation, revelation loses. For example, the Bible teaches that the first five books—Genesis, Exodus, Leviticus, Numbers, and Deuteronomy—were written by one man, Moses. The Jews referred to these books as the Law of Moses. Today we call them the Pentateuch, which means "five."

But about a hundred years ago, a group of men came along who called themselves rationalists. They said, in effect, "Our philosophy is that only that which is rational to the human intellect is true. If something cannot fit into our minds and be conceived by us to be true, it is not true."

They took a look at the Pentateuch and said, "Oh, oh. There are several things here we just can't understand. We don't agree that Moses wrote the first five books because the evolution of law came much later in history. He could never have written the Ten Commandments that early." So they said that Moses did not write Genesis through Deuteronomy.

Then who did? "Well, some fellows we'll refer to as *J, E, P,* and *D* did. You see, whenever the name Jehovah is used for God in the text, that means that the *J* writer was at work. And when the *Elohim* name for God is used, that's a mark of the *E* writer. And we've assigned *P* for the efforts of the Priestly writer, and *D* for the one who wrote Deuteronomy."

One problem with that position, incidentally, is that sometimes the work of *J, E, P,* and *D* all show up in the same verse! As for Moses not being able to give the Law, historians have discovered the Code of Hammurabi, a very sophisticated legal system that *predates* Moses.

Out With Creation, In With Evolution. For another example of how philosophy nullifies revelation, consider the Bible teaching that God is the creator of all things. Genesis 1:1 tells us, "In the beginning God created the heaven and the earth." On the first day, the second day, the third day, the fourth day, the fifth day, and the sixth day, God created. And on the seventh day, God rested. The Bible is very explicit that God created.

"Oh, no," says human philosophy. "Actually, the only explanation for the existence of things is evolution." Evolutionists go on to explain that once upon a time there was a primeval puddle. And in this primeval puddle was a one-celled thing that was very, very distressed about being all alone. It wanted company, so it split and became two. And then, of course, everything went wild, and here we are! That, in a nutshell, is a very limited scientific explanation of evolution.

Does the Bible say anything about evolution? No, the word doesn't appear in Scripture at all. Human philosophy speaks of evolution, but the Word of God does not.

Now there are some people who can't swallow the puddle story but neither can they accept the Bible account that God completed all of creation in six days. So they say, "We believe in theistic evolution. We'll have a conglomerate of both. God made the puddle, and then it evolved until man arrived. At that point God zapped man with a soul." Once again, philosophy imposes itself on revelation, and revelation is the loser. We don't need evolution, and God certainly doesn't need it.

Battling the Bible. For another illustration, take the field of psychology. The Bible tells us how to live. It says the way to get rid of guilt is to confess sin. I know of no better way. I can't name one psychiatrist who can deliver anybody from sin. Yet some who are familiar with the Bible go off to universities and study Freud for several years. Then they try to mix psychology and the Bible and guess which loses? The Bible. God did not need Freud. Freud needed God.

Someone else comes along and says, "I know the Bible teaches the Gospel, but we must add to the Gospel." And they create what is known as the "social gospel." And pretty soon the true Gospel is lost.

Others who seem to be working within the framework of religion actually pull the rug out from under biblical Christianity. One example is Rudolph Bultmann. Bultmann sought to "demythologize" Scripture. That means he wanted to take out all the "myths" of the Bible. And what is a myth? Anything that Bultmann didn't believe. Bultmann's philosophy imposed upon revelation, and once again revelation lost.

His or Ours. Revelation doesn't need philosophy of any kind. You don't need philosophy. You don't need human wisdom. If you know the Word of God and understand it, you have the reason for everything. You understand what you need to know, and you have solutions to your problems.

In the final analysis, there are only two views of life—God's and man's. That which makes man the center ends in indulgence, shallowness, and shortsightedness. The man-centered view is unrealistic, panders to the flesh, elevates desire, supports pride, and advocates independence. As Romans 1:25 says, it changes the truth of God into a lie and worships the creature more than the Creator. That is the result of human philosophy.

Now what is the antithesis of human philosophy? What does God's revelation set forth as man's great need? The cross of Jesus Christ. The central message of the Bible is quite simple. It declares that God in the person of Jesus Christ died on a cross and paid the penalty for sin. And now anyone who accepts that truth can be saved and have his eternal destiny secured in heaven forever.

Many people who hear that proclamation say, "That's ridiculous. We can't buy it. That idea is foolish. It's stupid." That is exactly the response predicted in 1 Corinthians 1:18: "For the preaching of the cross is to them that perish foolishness; but unto us which are saved it is the power of God."

So here is the great conflict—the word of the cross versus the word of human wisdom. The word of the cross in this context means all that is involved in the cross—the total revelation of God. The entire Bible is the word of the cross. Everything in the Bible before the cross points to it, and everything in the Bible after the cross explains it. Everything that God has to say to us, then, culminates in the cross of Jesus Christ.

And what is the future of human wisdom? The Word of God tells us: ". . . the wisdom of their wise men shall perish, and the understanding of their prudent men shall be hid" (Isaiah 29:14). The day is coming when all the philosophies of men shall be swept away, when all of man's wisdom will become ashes. Then Christ alone will reign as King of Kings.

Jeremiah 8:9 raises a vital issue: "The wise men are ashamed, they are dismayed and taken: lo, they have rejected the word of the Lord; and what wisdom is in them?" If a person rejects God's revelation, what wisdom is left to him? None. God is set against worldly wisdom. He destroys it.

The kind of human wisdom I am talking about is best defined in the Bible in James 3:15: "This wisdom descendeth not from above, but is earthly, sensual, devilish." Human wisdom is earthly in that it never gets beyond this tangible world; it never really understands divine supernatural reality.

Human wisdom is sensual in that it is based on human desire and lust. And human wisdom is demonic in that its source is Satan and/or it plays into the hands of Satan.

Now what can that kind of wisdom accomplish? Not very much. Throughout history human wisdom has never solved our real problems.

"But wait a minute," someone objects, "we used to be living out in the bush but now we're residing in condominiums and penthouse suites."

Yes, but we are just as sinful now as in the past. Human wisdom has only made us more comfortable with our problems.

What has philosophy ever contributed to man? What has it ever done to make him nobler, to make him a better person in his heart? Nothing. The wisdom of this world is stupidity when it tries to redeem men, when it tries to transform sinners. Philosophy never gets to the real issue of dealing with man's eternal soul. It falls short of what should be its great objective, the knowledge of God. Human philosophy never meets God and never experiences His peace, joy, forgiveness, freedom from guilt, meaning to life, and eternal hope.

So God moved in to do what human wisdom could not accomplish: "For after that in the wisdom of God the world by wisdom knew not God, it pleased God by the foolishness of preaching to save them that believe" (1 Corinthians 1:21). What man's wisdom could never do, God did through the cross. And the way it becomes effective in our lives is through belief in the revealed Word.

Sometimes It Is Hard to Get a Conviction. But that belief is not what all who claim to be Christians believe. They question whether the Bible is without error, completely infallible in every detail and singularly authoritative. Among many so-called Christians there is a lack of conviction about the Scripture. J. I. Packer comments on this in the book *God Has Spoken:*

Certainty about the great issues of Christian faith and con-
duct is lacking all along the line. The outside observer sees us
as staggering on from gimmick to gimmick and stunt to stunt
like so many drunks in a fog, not knowing at all where we are
or which way we should be going. Preaching is hazy; heads
are muddled; hearts fret; doubts drain our strength; uncer-
tainty paralyses action. We know the Victorian shibboleth that
to travel hopefully is better than to arrive and it leaves us cold.
Ecclesiastics of a certain type tell us that the wish to be certain is mere weakness of the flesh, a sign of spiritual immatu-
rity, but we do not find ourselves able to believe them. We
know in our bones that we were made for certainty, and we
cannot be happy without it. Yet, unlike the first Christians
who in three centuries won the Roman world, and those later
Christians who pioneered the Reformation, and the Puritan
awakening, and the Evangelical revival, and the great mis-
sionary movement of the last century, we lack certainty. Why
is this? We blame the external pressures of modern sec-
ularism, but this is like Eve blaming the serpent. The real
trouble is not in our circumstances, but in ourselves.

How tragic! Self-styled man has decided that his own intel-
lectualism is the answer to everything. Our Christian society
has become a swirl of self-centered deciders who will determine for themselves what truth is.

The result is that the Word of God is lost. The Prophet Amos
spoke of a similar scene: "Behold, the days come, saith the
Lord God, that I will send a famine in the land, not a famine of
bread, nor a thirst for water, but of hearing the words of the
Lord" (Amos 8:11).

Amos even goes on to describe the spiritual destitution that
results when you don't love the Word of the Lord. He pictures
frantic souls wandering everywhere, listening with hopes of
hearing God's voice—but it is never heard (*see* verse 12).

In the past years of the church the legacy of liberalism,
denominationalism, programism, and social activity has been
a loss of God's Word. But that is changing. There is a new

thrust of Bible study and teaching in the land. Christians are again renewing the age-old orthodox view of Scripture.

This book is offered with the prayer that it will be one of many catalysts to end the famine of the Word and stimulate the confidence of God's people in God's matchless Book—the Bible.